The Prayer

and its Effect in Increasing *Eemaan* and Purifying the Soul

By
Shaykh Husayn al-'Awaayishah

Translated by
Aboo Talhah Daawood ibn Ronald Burbank

ISBN 1 898649 13 8

British Library Cataloguing in Publication Data.

A catalogue record for this book is available from the British Library.

First Edition, 1416 AH/1995 CE

Cover design: Abu Yahya

Printed by: All Trade Printers, Birmingham, U.K.

Typeset by: Al-Hidaayah Publishing and Distribution

Published by: Al-Hidaayah Publishing and Distribution
P.O. Box 3332
Birmingham
United Kingdom
B10 9AW

Tel: 0121 753 1889
Fax: 0121 753 2422

Publisher's Note

All praise is due to Allaah, Lord of the worlds. Peace and blessings of Allaah be upon Muhammad, his family, his Companions and all those who follow in their footsteps until the Last Day.

The Prayer has become bothersome and unimportant to many of us. Instead the Muslims have preoccupied themselves with more 'important' things, spending all their time in these other matters and yet constantly finding that they are unable to reap the fruits of their labour. Frantically they search for causes and examine all their affairs - except that which is the closest to them, the Prayer.

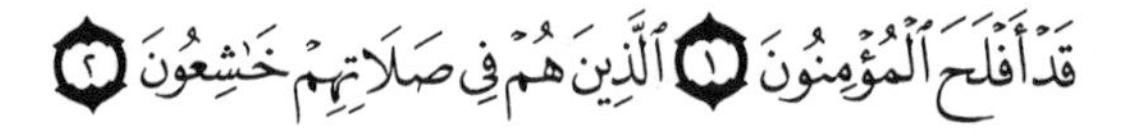

"Successful indeed are the believers. Those who offer their Prayers with humility and attentiveness."

Soorah al-Mu'minoon (23):1-2

Whether we are desperate for success or would welcome the thought of it, few of us recognize that the manner in which we perform our Prayer in-fact determines whether or not we will taste the sweetness of this true success.

Before you is a most distinguished, heart rendering book entitled *The Prayer, its Effect in Increasing Eemaan and Purifying the Soul*, (an English translation of the Arabic book: *As-Salaat, wa Athruhaa fee Ziyaadatil Eemaan wa Tahdheebun Nafs*) by Shaykh Husayn al-'Awaayishah. Books of this nature are very few and this particular work has been long overdue and eagerly awaited in the English language. The author discusses at length many issues pertaining to perfecting the Prayer and how humility and attentiveness are to be achieved, and how that leads to tranquillity and peace of mind, and causes the abandonment of sins and purifies the soul.

This poignant book is concerned with the Muslims' well being, and our Shaykh has scrutinized the illness of this *Ummah* and expended much of his time in and effort to search for the precise cure - indeed it is the Prayer.

"O Muslim! *The Prayer, the Prayer*, the last thing which the Prophet (ﷺ) said, and the first thing which the servant will be accountable for on the Day of Resurrection. So fear Allaah with regard to your own souls, and take account of yourselves before you are taken to account."

Al-Hidaayah Publishing and Distribution.

Note: All references quoted refer to the Arabic books unless otherwise stated.

Contents

بِسْمِ ٱللَّهِ ٱلرَّحْمَٰنِ ٱلرَّحِيمِ

Introduction

Indeed all praise is for Allaah, we praise Him, we seek His help and ask for His forgiveness. We seek Allaah's refuge from the evils of ourselves and from our evil actions. Whomsoever Allaah guides none can misguide him, and whomsoever Allaah misguides none can guide him. I bear witness that none has the right to be worshipped except Allaah, alone, having no partner, and I bear witness that Muhammad is His slave and His Messenger.

يَٰٓأَيُّهَا ٱلَّذِينَ ءَامَنُوا۟ ٱتَّقُوا۟ ٱللَّهَ حَقَّ تُقَاتِهِۦ وَلَا تَمُوتُنَّ إِلَّا وَأَنتُم مُّسْلِمُونَ

"O you who believe! Fear Allaah as He should be feared. And die not except in a state of Islam (as Muslims)."[1]

يَٰٓأَيُّهَا ٱلنَّاسُ ٱتَّقُوا۟ رَبَّكُمُ ٱلَّذِى خَلَقَكُم مِّن نَّفْسٍ وَٰحِدَةٍ وَخَلَقَ مِنْهَا
زَوْجَهَا وَبَثَّ مِنْهُمَا رِجَالًا كَثِيرًا وَنِسَآءً ۚ وَٱتَّقُوا۟ ٱللَّهَ ٱلَّذِى تَسَآءَلُونَ
بِهِۦ وَٱلْأَرْحَامَ ۚ إِنَّ ٱللَّهَ كَانَ عَلَيْكُمْ رَقِيبًا ﴿١﴾

"O mankind be dutiful to your Lord, who created you from a single person (Aadam), and from him He created his wife, and from them both He created many men and women. Fear Allaah through whom you demand your mutual (rights), and (do not cut the relations of) the wombs (kinship). Surely, Allaah is ever an All Watcher over you."[2]

---

[1] Soorah Aal-'Imraan (3):102

[2] Soorah an-Nisaa' (4):1

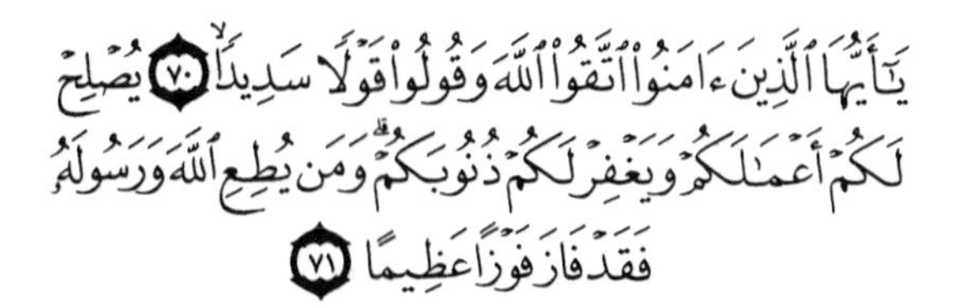

" O you who believe! Keep your duty to Allaah and fear Him, and speak (always) the truth. He will direct you to do righteous good deeds and will forgive you your sins. And whosoever obeys Allaah and His Messenger, he has indeed achieved a great achievement."[3]

To proceed: The truest speech is the Book of Allaah, and the best way is the way of Muhammad (ﷺ). The worst of affairs are the novelties, every novelty is an innovation, every innovation is misguidance, and misguidance is in the Fire.

The people have indeed come to treat the Prayer as something unimportant. Attentiveness and humility in it have been taken away, except from those whom Allaah, the Most High, wills. The hearts have become darkened and the people's distressed state has become grave. They have searched for the causes and strive to find a cure, but are unable to find it. They have looked into everything except their Prayers, which are the closest of affairs to them.

'Like the dusky camel in the desert killed by the man suffering from thirst, whilst water is carried upon its back.' The Prayer used to be a source of delight for the Prophet (ﷺ) and of tranquillity for his soul.[4] So what is wrong with us that we seek after tranquillity and success in matters which will only weary us and bring us grief?

---

[3] Soorah al-Ahzaab (33):70-71

[4] The *ahaadeeth* about this will be quoted in their due place in the book, if Allaah wills.

Indeed the well being of the soul begins with rectification of one's belief (*'aqeedah*) and one's Prayer, and I do not think that I am exaggerating when I say that correct Prayer done with full attentiveness and humility is one of the most important means for the success and victory of this *Ummah*.[5]

Prayer is furthermore, a mirror of the Muslim's actions. If it is in a good state then the rest of his actions will be likewise, whereas if it is in a bad state then the rest of his actions will be in a similar condition.[6]

Because the noble Companions *radiyallaahu 'anhum*, understood the excellence of Prayer, and their hearts and bodies submitted with full humility and attention, and their behaviour was good and their manners refined, they attained honour and leadership. Whereas we complain of being defeated, crushed, and of people's evil. We complain about those related to us and those whom we love. A person even complains about his ownself. Should he not be complaining about his enemies?!

So let us reflect upon our Prayer and compare it with the Prayer of the Prophet (ﷺ) and his Companions, *radiyallaahu 'anhum*, since that is the way to change the souls and turn them to that which is more lofty. That is the way to success, well being and salvation in this life and the Hereafter.

I decided to write about the Prayer due to this conviction, and to write at some length. Hence I examined the relevant texts, the *Aayaat* and the *ahaadeeth* and I referred back to the works of *tafseer* and sayings of the scholars about them, as far as I was able. Then I considered carefully what would be of the greatest benefit and use, and what could be derived from

---

[5] The *ahaadeeth* about this will be quoted in their due place in the book, if Allaah wills.

[6] The *ahaadeeth* about this will be quoted in their due place in the book, if Allaah wills.

it, considering the illness and searching for the precise cure relevant to practical life. I compiled it hoping that Allaah will guide me to and grant me correctness and success. I ask Allaah, the One free and far removed from all defects, and the Most High, to make my action purely for His Noble Face, and that He makes it of benefit to myself and my Muslim brothers in all corners of the world, and that He makes it something from which I derive benefit after actions have been cut off, when one's appointed time has been reached. Indeed He has Power over everything.

(1) What is Obligatory Upon the Muslim in His Prayer

One of the greatest of the affairs that will increase the *eemaan*[7] of the Muslim is the Prayer. He, the One free and far removed from all defects, says:

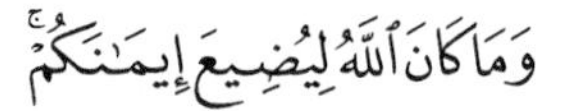

> **"... and Allaah would never make your *eemaan* (Prayers) to be lost..."**[8]

Meaning: Your Prayer offered in the direction of Jerusalem.[9, 10]

Also in the *hadeeth*: *I order you with four, and forbid you from four: I order you to have Faith in Allaah alone. Do you know what is having Faith in Allaah alone? The testification that none has the right to be worshipped except Allaah, and that Muhammad is the Messenger of Allaah, and that you establish the Prayer, give the Zakaat, fast in Ramadaan, and that you give one fifth of the war-booty. I forbid you from four: the hollowed gourd, wooden pots, varnished wine jars and pitch-smeared wine containers.11 Remember these and inform those whom you have left behind of them.*[12]

---

[7] Translator's note: *Eemaan* being true Islamic faith comprising correct belief, words and actions.

[8] Soorah al-Baqarah (2):143

[9] See *Saheehul-Bukhaaree* (Eng. trans 1/34-35,/chapter 31)

[10] Translator's note: So Allaah referred to Prayer as *eemaan*.

[11] Translator's note: These were all containers in which wine was prepared, carried or drunk see *Fathul-Baaree* (1/134-135).

[12] Reported by al-Bukhaaree (Eng. trans. 1/45/no.50), and Muslim (Eng. trans 1/11/no.22) and others.

So the Muslim must administer great care and attention with regards to his Prayer, by taking care of the following matters:

(i) The Prayer Should, to the Best of One's Ability, Comply with the Prayer of the Prophet (ﷺ)

This will be attained by referring to the chapters of Prayer in the books of *hadeeth* and *fiqh.*[13] For when that is the case the Muslim worshipper, when performing the actions, pillars and obligations of the Prayer will be conscious that he is following the way of the Prophet (ﷺ). In this way he shall begin to abandon what he (ﷺ) abandoned, and do sometimes, whatever the Prophet (ﷺ) did sometimes. He will also vary the *adhkaar* which he says in his Prayer when it is found that there are different things authentically reported from him (ﷺ). So for example, sometimes using one, and at other times using another, just as he (ﷺ) did.

In this way the person will feel that he is following the footsteps of the Prophet (ﷺ) and will taste the sweetness of following and obeying him. What love can be greater than following the Prophet (ﷺ) since it is the one and only path towards Allaah, the One free of all imperfections and the Most High?

From Aboo Ayyoob *radiyallaahu 'anhu* who said that I heard Allaah's Messenger (ﷺ) say: *Whoever makes wudoo as he has been ordered, and prays as he has been ordered, then whatever action he had done previously is forgiven for him.*[14]

---

[13] One of the best books that I have seen in this regard is the book *The Prophet's Prayer Described from the beginning to the end as though you see it* of Shaikh Muhammad Naasirudeen al-Albaanee *hafidhahullaah*, which he compiled using material from 163 source books and manuscripts.

[14] Reported by an-Nasaa'ee, ad-Daarimee, Ahmad, Ibn Maajah and Ibn Hibbaan in his *Saheeh*, except that his wording is: *...his previous sins are forbidden.* See *Saheehut-Targheeb wat-Tarheeb* (no.191).

There occurs in the *hadeeth* of Maalik ibn al-Huwayrith *radiyallaahu 'anhu*, from the Prophet (ﷺ) that he said: *Pray just as you have seen me praying.*[15]

From 'Ammaar ibn Yaasir *radiyallaahu 'anhu*, who said Allaah's Messenger (ﷺ) said: *A man may return (after Prayer) and only a tenth of his Prayer, or a ninth, or an eighth, or a seventh, or a sixth, or a fifth, or a quarter, or a third, or half of it is written for him.*[16]

(ii) One Should have *Khushoo'*[17] in the Prayer

Allaah, the One free of all imperfections and the Most High, says:

قَدْ أَفْلَحَ ٱلْمُؤْمِنُونَ ﴿١﴾ ٱلَّذِينَ هُمْ فِى صَلَاتِهِمْ خَٰشِعُونَ ﴿٢﴾

"Successful indeed are the believers. Those who offer their Prayers with humility and attentiveness (*khushoo'*)."[18]

---

[15] Part of a *hadeeth* reported by al-Bukhaaree (Eng. trans. 1/345/no.604) and Ahmad.

[16] Reported by Ahmad, Aboo Daawood (Eng. trans. 1/203/no.789), and Ibn Hibbaan who declared it *saheeh* and it is in *Saheehul-Jaami'* (no.622).

[17] Translator's note: The term *khushoo'* occurs frequently throughout the book and is usually translated as 'humility and attentiveness'. Ibn Hajr explained it in *Fathul-Baaree* (2/225) saying: *"Khushoo' is sometimes an action of the heart, like fear, and sometimes of the body, like calmness/stillness and it is said: Both of them must be present... Others say: It is something found in the soul which manifests itself in stillness of the body parts and agrees with what is required from worship..."*

[18] Soorah al-Mu'minoon (23):1-2

He, the Most Perfect, says:

وَقُومُواْ لِلَّهِ قَٰنِتِينَ ﴿٢٣٨﴾

"And stand before Allaah with obedience."[19]

From Aboo Hurairah *radiyallaahu 'anhu* who said that Allaah's Messenger (ﷺ) prayed one day, then afterwards turned and said: *O so and so will you not perfect your Prayer? Will the person seeing not see how he prays? Indeed he prays it for himself.*[20]

This shall be attained through observing a number of matters, some of them are within the Prayer itself and some are outside it, and from among them is:

(a) Remembrance of death

From Anas *radiyallaahu 'anhu*, who said that Allaah's Messenger (ﷺ) said: *Remember death in your Prayers, since if a person remembers death in his Prayer he will be likely to pray well. Pray the Prayer of a man who*

---

[19] Soorah al-Baqarah (2):238.
Ibn Katheer says in his *Tafseer*: "Meaning: humbly and submissively." There occurs in *Saheeh Muslim* (Eng. trans. 1/272/no.1098) from Zayd ibn Arqam *radiyallaahu 'anhu*, who said: *We used to talk while praying, a person would speak to his companion at his side until it was revealed:*

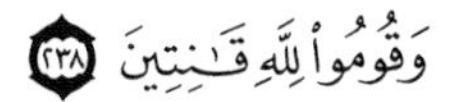

"And stand before Allaah with obedience."
[Soorah al-Baqarah (2):238]

So we were ordered to be silent and forbidden from speaking.

[20] Reported by Muslim [Eng. trans. 1/235/no.853].

does not think he will pray another Prayer besides it, and beware of every matter which requires excuse.[21]

So Allaah's Messenger (ﷺ) ordered the Muslim to remember death in his Prayer since it will cause him to perfect his Prayer since death causes fear in the souls and with it one's actions are sealed, and what comes after it is even more fearful and fear inducing. For is there a place where one can flee to, to escape from the constriction suffered in the grave? What will our reply be when we are questioned in the grave? Indeed not a single one of us knows where we will end up. Will it be the Paradise whose width is like the heavens and the earth, or shall it be the Fire whose fuel is men and stones?

In his mind this is how the Muslim should picture death and what is to come after it. For then he prays like a man who does not think that he will pray another Prayer besides it. So he will perfect his Prayer, be sincere in repentance and will count himself amongst the dead, preparing his shroud, writing his will, fulfilling anything due upon him from the people. In the morning he does not await the evening, and in the evening he does not await the morning.

Hence this is the manner in which he approaches the Prayer, with utmost humility and concentration, weeping, between fear and hope before the Hereafter, saying farewell to this world. It should be the Prayer for one saying farewell, and a final Prayer. It is the Prayer of one saying farewell to his family, his parents, his brothers, those whom he loves and his relations, indeed to the whole world.

---

[21] Reported by ad-Daylamee in *Musnadul-Firdaws* and declared *hasan* by Shaikh al-Albaanee in *Saheehul-Jaami'* (no.862).

When saying *Allaahu Akbar* (Allaah is greater) he declares that Allaah is greater than everything and he declares the insignificance of this worldly life. Then he supplicates with one of the opening supplications. Thus when he says:

"O Allaah separate me from my sins as you have separated the east from the west", then he thinks of the distance between the east and the west, and of the sins which weigh heavily upon his back and he fears that he should meet Allaah, the One free and far removed from all imperfections, in that state, and that his life should end without having repented. He supplicates with this supplication, being certain that he shall be answered. Likewise he considers the meaning of everything in his Prayer, and keeps the remembrance of the Greatness of Allaah, the Most High, in his heart. He is found weeping and shedding tears since Paradise and the Hell-Fire seem closer to him than the strap of his shoe. He is a visible example of his (ﷺ) saying: *Pray the Prayer of one who is bidding farewell, as if you were seeing Him (Allaah). For even though you do not see Him, yet He certainly sees you.*[22]

One must be mindful of Allaah, the Most High, in the Prayer in order for the Prayer to be perfected. We must place the world behind our backs. Indeed how would it be if the person knew that his words were being listened to, and that they were definitely going to reach the ruler, then what would he say? How would he speak? Do you not think that he would carefully consider each word and each letter that he utters? Then how about the one who stands before the All-Hearing, All-Seeing and All-Knowing, the One from Whom nothing is hidden?

---

[22] *Hasan* see *Saheehul-Jaami'* (no.3670).

The Prophet (ﷺ) used to pray and the sound of weeping, like the sound of a pot when boiling would be heard emanating from his chest out of his awe and veneration of Allaah, the One free and far removed of all defects.

'Abdullaah ibn ash-Shikhkheer *radiyallaahu 'anhu*, said: *I saw Allaah's Messenger (ﷺ) leading us in Prayer and a sound like the boiling of a pot could be heard emanating from his chest due to weeping.*[23]

The weeping of 'Umar *radiyallaahu 'anhu*, was such that it could be heard by those in the last row, as occurs in al-Bukhaaree. This is what is reported by 'Abdullaah ibn Shaddaad who said: *I heard the weeping of 'Umar and I was in the last of the rows and he was reciting:*

قَالَ إِنَّمَآ أَشْكُواْ بَثِّى وَحُزْنِىٓ إِلَى ٱللَّهِ

"...I only complain of my grief and sorrow to Allaah..." [Soorah Yoosuf (12):86] [24]

As for Aboo Bakr *radiyallaahu 'anhu*, then the people were unable to hear his recitation in Prayer due to his weeping as 'Aa'ishah *radiyallaahu 'anhaa*, reported, saying: *In his (final) illness the Messenger of Allaah (ﷺ) said: Order Aboo Bakr to lead the people in Prayer. So 'Aa'ishah said: When Aboo Bakr stands in your place the people are unable to*

---

[23] Reported by Aboo Daawood [Eng. trans. 1/230/no.903] and others. Al-Haafidh Ibn Hajr said in *al-Fath*: "Its chain of narration is strong." It was also declared *saheeh* by Ibn Khuzaimah, Ibn Hibbaan and al-Haakim.

[24] Reported by al-Bukhaaree [Eng. trans. 1/385/chapt.69]. Al-Haafidh Ibn Hajr quotes in *Fathul-Baaree* from Ibn Faaris that the word used for 'weeping' here, indicates weeping which one keeps in the throat and does not reach the level of weeping openly without restraint. Al-Harawee said that it meant a quivering noise like the weeping of a child which breaks through repeatedly from the chest, and it is said in *al-Muhkam*: *It is the severest weeping.*

hear him due to his weeping so order 'Umar to lead the people in Prayer. So he (ﷺ) said: Order Aboo Bakr to lead the people in Prayer. 'Aa'ishah said to Hafsah: Say to him that if Aboo Bakr stands in your place then the people will not be able to hear him due to his weeping, so order 'Umar to lead the people in Prayer. So Hafsah did so, so Allaah's Messenger (ﷺ) said: Desist. Indeed you are (like) the companions of Yoosuf. Order Aboo Bakr to lead the people in Prayer. Hafsah said to 'Aa'ishah: I never attained good from you.[25]

And in another narration: *Aboo Bakr is a soft-hearted man and would not be able to lead the people in Prayer standing in your place.*[26]

(b) Reflecting on the words which one says in the Prayer

When he recites *Allaahu Akbar* (Allaah is greater) he remembers its meaning and the declaration of Allaah's greatness that it comprises. Then when he seeks Allaah's refuge he considers its meaning and understands that he is seeking the protection of Allaah, the All-Hearing, who Hears His servant, and the All-Knowing, who Knows what the devils whisper and suggest. He comprehends that through it he opens the door to all good, and closes the doors to every evil... likewise he considers the meanings of *Bismillaah...*, of the *Tasbeeh* and of his sending *Salaat* upon the Prophet (ﷺ). In order to achieve this he must refer to the books of *Tafseer* and sayings of the scholars in this regard so that he can understand what he is saying and say what he understands, and that applies to all of his Prayer in which he should strive against his own self as far as he is able.

---

[25] Al-Bukhaaree [Eng. trans.1/386/no.684].

[26] Reported by al-Bukhaaree [Eng. trans. 1/358/no.633].

(c) Abandoning sins

Allaah, the One free and far removed from all imperfections, says:

إِنَّ ٱللَّهَ لَا يُغَيِّرُ مَا بِقَوْمٍ حَتَّىٰ يُغَيِّرُوا۟ مَا بِأَنفُسِهِمْ

> **"Verily Allaah will not change the condition of a people as long as they do not change what is within themselves."**[27]

Sins are a substantial obstacle hindering the way to attainment of concentration and humility (*khushoo'*) in the Prayer. From them is that a man remains married to a woman of evil character and does not divorce her, or that he gives wealth to those lacking in intellect, or makes a loan to someone without witnesses. This is due to what is established from the Prophet (ﷺ) that he said: *There are three who call upon Allaah, the Mighty and Majestic, and they are not responded to: A man married to a woman of evil character and he does not divorce her, and a man who has wealth held by another but he does not get that witnessed, and a man who gives wealth to one lacking in intellect, and Allaah, the Most High, says:*

وَلَا تُؤْتُوا۟ ٱلسُّفَهَآءَ أَمْوَٰلَكُمُ

> **"And give not unto the foolish your property..."**[28, 29]

---

[27] Soorah ar-Ra'd (13):11

[28] Soorah an-Nisaa' (4):5

[29] Reported by al-Haakim from Aboo Moosa, and it is found in *Saheehul-Jaami'* (no.3070).

Likewise a wife's disobedience to her husband and a slave fleeing from his owner, as occurs in the *hadeeth*: *There are two whose Prayer does not ascend above their heads: A slave who flees from his owner until he returns, and a woman who disobeys her husband until she returns (to obedience).*[30]

Whereas as increasing in acts of obedience causes the Prayer to become more perfect and enables the person to pray with humility and concentration. From among these actions is: having mercy upon the orphan and stroking his head, and feeding him. Concerning this the Prophet (ﷺ) said: *Do you love that your heart should become soft and that you should be successful in what you seek after? Be merciful to the orphan, stroke his head and feed him with your food, your heart will become soft, and you will be successful in what you seek after.*[31]

(d) Avoidance of excessive laughter since it kills off the heart and empties it of humility (*khushoo'*)

As occurs in the *hadeeth*: *...excessive laughter kills the heart.*[32]

(e) Choosing suitable work

A number of matters need to be taken into account:

(i) That it is something lawful, since Allaah, the Most High, accepts only that which is pure, and the supplication of one who eats forbidden wealth is rejected and he is deprived of humility (*khushoo'*).

---

[30] Reported by al-Haakim from Ibn 'Umar see *Saheehul-Jaami'* (no.135).

[31] Reported by at-Tabaraanee from Abud-Dardaa see *Saheehul-Jaami'* (no.80).

[32] Reported by Imaam Ahmad, at-Tirmidhee and others and it is found in *Saheehul-Jaami'* (no.99).

(ii) That this work does not conflict with the times of Prayer, since if this is the case then the person will make allowance for himself to delay the Prayers or to pray them outside their times, either due to his own negligence or because he manages to find someone who declares that to be lawful for him.

(iii) That he should, as far as he is able, search for work that is not extremely strenuous, so that when he comes to pray he is able to turn penitent to his Lord with a humble and attentive heart. For the one who is over worked and exhausted will not be able to concentrate which will in turn reduce his humility and attentiveness in Prayer. The Prophet (ﷺ) ordered that when a person's evening meal is placed before him and the *iqaamah* is pronounced that one should start with the evening meal until one finishes. This is so that one may remove anything which will take one's attention away from the Prayer. Ibn 'Umar *radiyallaahu 'anhumaa*, reports that the Prophet (ﷺ) said: *If the evening meal of one of you is placed before him and the Iqaamah is given for the Prayer then begin with the evening meal, and do not hasten in finishing it.*[33]

(f) Avoiding being preoccupied with this world

Indeed this will certainly be to the detriment of one's Hereafter. Rather one should take from this world what is sufficient to cover oneself, one's wife and one's children. So if the work which you do in the morning suffices you, then there is no need to work in the afternoon. Then if you are granted success in a particular business which yields good profits, then there is no need to become involved in other business ventures which shall only take a further share of your attention and cause you to forget the rights of your Lord, your ownself, your wife and your family.

---

[33] Reported by al-Bukhaaree (Eng. trans. 1/362/no.642) and Muslim (Eng. trans. 1/278/no.1137).

(g) Frequently reciting the Noble Qur'aan

Frequently recting the Noble Qur'aan and also authentic *adhkaar* and supplications, and reading such things as will soften the heart and repel Satan.

(h) Coming to Prayer in good time (early)

It is important to come to the Prayer early so that your desire to reach the Prayer does not cause you to have to hurry, for then you enter into Prayer in a flustered and agitated state. From Aboo Qataadah *radiyallaahu 'anhu*, who said that Allaah's Messenger (ﷺ) said: *When you come to the Prayer, then come with calmness, and do not come hurrying. So whatever you reach then pray it, and whatever you miss then complete it.*[34]

From Aboo Hurairah *radiyallaahu 'anhu*, who said that Allaah's Messenger (ﷺ) said: *When the iqaamah for the Prayer is given then do not run to it but come to it with calmness. Then pray whatever you reach and make up whatever you miss, since when one of you is proceeding to the Prayer he is infact in Prayer.*[35]

(i) Straightening the rows and standing closely together

This is because gaps are the places where Satan stands, as occurs in the *hadeeth*: *Stand closer together in the rows, since Satan stands in the gaps.*[36]

---

[34] Reported by Ahmad, al-Bukhaaree (Eng. trans. 1/347/no.608), and Muslim (Eng. trans. 1/297/no.1253).

[35] Reported by Muslim (Eng. trans. 1/296/no.1250)

[36] Reported by Ahmad and Aboo Daawood (Eng. trans. 1/173/no.167) and it is found in *Saheehul-Jaami'* (no.3448).

He (ﷺ) used to say with regards to the straightening of the rows: *Be straight and do not be irregular for your hearts would then disagree.*[37] He (ﷺ) also used to say: *You must straighten your rows or Allaah will alter your faces.*[38]

Thus failing to straighten the rows causes alteration in and dissension between the faces and the hearts. It reduces *eemaan* and kills off humility and attentiveness. Likewise straightening the rows is from the completion and perfection of the Prayer as the Prophet (ﷺ) said: ... *since straightening the rows is part of the completion of the Prayer.*[39] He (ﷺ) said: ... *since the straightening of the row is amongst those things which make the Prayer perfect.*[40]

(iii) Praying Within the Stated Time

Allaah, the Most High, says:

إِنَّ ٱلصَّلَوٰةَ كَانَتْ عَلَى ٱلْمُؤْمِنِينَ كِتَٰبًا مَّوْقُوتًا ﴿١٠٣﴾

> **"Verily, the Prayer is enjoined on the believers at fixed hours."**[41]

Al-Bukhaaree *rahimahullaahu ta'aalaa*, said in explanation of this: "Prescribed at fixed times for them."

---

[37] Reported by Ahmad, Muslim (Eng. trans. 1/238/no.868) and others.

[38] Reported by al-Bukhaaree (Eng. trans. 1/386/no.685).

[39] Reported by Muslim (Eng. trans. 1/238/no.871).

[40] Reported by al-Bukhaaree (Eng. trans. 1/388/no.689).

[41] Soorah an-Nisaa' (4):103.

From Aboo 'Amr ash-Shaybaanee who said: "The occupants of this house, and he pointed to the house of 'Abdullaah [i.e. Ibn Mas'ood], narrated to us, saying: *I asked the Prophet (ﷺ) which action is most beloved to Allaah? He replied: Prayer in its time. He said: What is next? He replied: Then to be good and dutiful to one's parents. He said: What is next? He replied: To participate in jihaad in Allaah's cause. He said: He narrated that to me and if I had asked him more he would have told me more.*"[42]

So Allaah's Messenger (ﷺ) explained that Prayer in its time is from the most beloved of actions, and he (ﷺ) gave it precedence over goodness and dutifulness to parents, and over *jihaad* in the way of Allaah. The proof for this is the word *thumma* (then) since it indicates order of precedence as is well-known in the Arabic language.

Al-Haafidh [Ibn Hajr] says in *Fathul-Baaree*:" Ibn Bazeezah said: 'Reflection would suggest giving precedence to *jihaad* over all actions of the body since it involves offering one's own life. However perservering in observing the Prayers within their times, and being constant in goodness and obedience to parents, are actions which are continual and are such that none but the true and sincere will manage to remember and fear Allaah concerning them, and Allaah knows best.'"

I will give an example to clarify what is meant: A man is totally preoccupied in his business and all that it entails and requires of him. Then Satan will often manage to deceive him so that he misses the initial *takbeer* or some of the Prayer. Then if you approach him with the texts about fighting *jihaad* in the cause of Allaah, the Most High, and give him examples of the bravery of the Companions *radiyallaahu 'anhum*, then they will indeed cause him to desire Paradise and to have less regard for this world.

---

[42] Reported by al-Bukhaaree (Eng. trans. 1/300/no.505) and others.

After you admonish him he will look at this world and find it less and less important, and he will look at the Hereafter and it will grow in importance in his eyes until he hastens towards the Paradise which is greater than the heavens and the earth. So he will hasten in writing his will, fulfil any rights the people have upon him and then bid farewell to his family and those whom he loves and go to the battlefield and be killed as a martyr in the cause of Allaah, the One free of all imperfections and the Most High. However if you did not call him to fight *jihaad* in the cause of Allaah, the Most High, but rather you called him to observe the Prayers upon their time, and you mentioned to him the relevant texts, the encouragement's and the warnings and reports which will have an effect upon him, then what do you think you will see as a result? Perhaps he will respond and weep over his previous actions and be determined to pray the Prayer on time. He will then, perhaps, do that for a few days but then Satan will start to whisper, his preoccupation's will increase. Commitments, engagements and appointments will mount up and Satan will strike at him, and he will sometimes fail to observe the Prayers as he should. Then he will again strive against his ownself and gain the upper hand over Satan. Then he will fall short again and so he will be in a continual struggle with Satan five times a day, and day after day for his whole life... So the first one strives against his own soul as does the second. But how is the first with regards to the second? The second strives for a whole lifetime, whereas the other strives for an hour, a few days, months or years. Whatever the case, I say: "In both there is good".

So I ask Allaah, the Most High, that He makes me one of those who are punctual in their Prayers with full humility and concentration, and in carrying out the rest of His orders, and that He writes me amongst the martyrs. Indeed He has full-power over everything.

From Mus'ab ibn Sa'd who said: "I said to my father: O my father! do you see his saying:

ٱلَّذِينَ هُمۡ عَن صَلَاتِهِمۡ سَاهُونَ

"Those who are neglectful of their Prayers."[43]

Which of us is never unmindful? Which of us never has his attention diverted? He said: That is not what is meant. Rather it is neglect of the times. A person becomes negligent to the point that he misses its time."[44]

From Moosa ibn Ismaa'eel who said that Mahdee narrated to us from Ghaylaan from Anas *radiyallaahu'anhu*, who said: I do not recognise anything that has remained from the time of the Prophet (ﷺ). It was said to him: The Prayer. He said: Have you not done regarding the Prayer what you have done [meaning: delaying the Prayer from its time]?[45]

From 'Uthmaan ibn Abee Rawaad the brother of 'Abdul-'Azeez who said that I heard az-Zuhree say: I entered upon Anas ibn Maalik in Damascus and he was weeping, so I said to him: What causes you to weep? He replied: I do not recognise anything which I used to know except this Prayer, and it itself is being lost.[46]

Al-Haafidh Ibn Hajr said in *Fathul-Baaree*: "Al-Muhallab said: What is meant by losing it is that they delayed it from its recommended time, not that they delayed it beyond its time altogether." However Ibn Hajr disagreed with this conclusion mentioning that what is correct is that they did delay the Prayer from its time. I say: The saying of the poet is most apt here: "They are two bitter things, the sweeter of the two is still bitter".

---

[43] Soorah al-Maa'oon (107):5

[44] Reported by Aboo Ya'laa with *hasan* chain of narration, and it is found in *Saheehut-Targheeb* (no.575).

[45] Reported by al-Bukhaaree (Eng. trans. 1/301/507).

[46] Reported by al-Bukhaaree (Eng. trans. 1/301/507).

So Anas *radiyallaahu 'anhu*, would weep, then what are we doing? What should we do? Is it not fitting that we should cause new seeds to spring up with our tears due to our negligence and neglect of the Prayer and the orders of Allaah, the Most High?!

From 'Ubaadah ibn as-Saamit *radiyallaahu 'anhu*, who said that I bear witness that I heard Allaah's Messenger (ﷺ) say: *Allaah, the Mighty and Majestic, has obligated five Prayers, whoever completes wudoo for them, prays them in their times, completes their rukoo' (bowing), sujood (prostration) and humility and concentration (khushoo'), then he has a guarantee from Allaah that He will forgive him. But whoever does not do that has no guarantee from Allaah: if He wishes He will forgive him, and if He wishes He will punish him.*[47]

From Ka'b ibn 'Ujrah *radiyallaahu 'anhu*, who said: *Allaah's Messenger came to us and we were seven in number; four from our freed-slaves and three Arabs, and we were resting our backs against his mosque, so he said: What has caused you to sit? We said: We are sitting waiting for the Prayer. So he remained silent for a while, then he turned to us and said: Do you know what your Lord says: We said: No. He said: Indeed your Lord says: Whoever prays the Prayer in its time and is constant in that, and does not neglect them and treat their rights lightly, then he has a guarantee from Me that I will enter him into Paradise. But whoever does not pray in its time, is not constant upon it, and neglects them treating their rights lightly, then he has no guarantee from Me. If I wish I will punish him, and if I wish I will forgive him.*[48]

---

[47] Reported by Maalik, Aboo Daawood (Eng. trans. 1/111/425), an-Nasaa'ee and declared *saheeh* by Ibn Hibbaan, and it is found in *Saheehut-Targheeb* (no.396).

[48] Reported by at-Tabaraanee in *al-Kabeer* and declared *saheeh* by Ibn Hibbaan and it is found in *Saheehut-Targheeb* (no.397).

From 'Abdullaah ibn Mas'ood *radiyallaahu 'anhu*, that the Prophet (ﷺ) passed by his Companions one day and said to them: *Do you know what your Lord, the Blessed and Most High, says? They said: Allaah and His Messenger know best. (He said it three times). He said: By My Might and My Majesty no one prays them in their times except that I will enter him into Paradise, and whoever prays them in other than their times then if I wish I will have mercy upon him, and if I wish I will punish him.*[49]

(iv) Praying in Congregation (*Jamaa'ah*)

Allaah, the Most High, says:

وَأَقِيمُواْ ٱلصَّلَوٰةَ وَءَاتُواْ ٱلزَّكَوٰةَ وَٱرۡكَعُواْ مَعَ ٱلرَّٰكِعِينَ ﴿٤٣﴾

> **"And offer perfectly the Prayers, and give *zakaat* and bow down with those that bow down."**[50]

Ibn Katheer said in his *Tafseer*: "He ordered them to bow in *rukoo'* along with those who bow in *rukoo'* from the *Ummah* of Muhammad (ﷺ) meaning: Be with them and from them," and he said: "Many of the scholars use this *Aayah* as a proof of the obligation of praying with the congregation (*Jamaa'ah*)."

From Abud-Dardaa *radiyallaahu 'anhu*, who said that Allaah's Messenger (ﷺ) said: *There are not three people in a town or in a desert place amongst whom the Prayer is not established, except that Satan gets the better of them. So cling to the Jamaa'ah for indeed the wolf devours the lone sheep.*[51]

---

[49] Reported by at-Tabaraanee in *al-Kabeer* and it is found in *Saheehut-Targheeb* (no.398).

[50] Soorah al-Baqarah (2):43

[51] Reported by Ahmad in his *Musnad*, Aboo Daawood (Eng. trans. 1/144/no.547) and others and it is found in *Saheehul-Jaami'* (no.5577).

There occurs in the *hadeeth*: *By Him in Whose Hand is my soul, I was about to order that firewood be collected, then order that the adhaan be given for the Prayer, and then order a man to lead the Prayer, and then I would go to those men who stayed away and burn down their houses upon them. By Him in Whose Hand is my soul, if one of them knew that he would find a bone covered with meat, or two small pieces of good meat, then he would have turned up for the 'Ishaa Prayer.*[52]

From 'Abdullaah ibn 'Umar *radiyallaahu 'anhu*, who said that Allaah's Messenger (ﷺ) said: *Prayer with the congregation is better than the Prayer of a person alone by twenty-seven times.*[53]

Al-A'mash said that I heard Saalim say that I heard Ummud-Dardaa say: "Abud-Dardaa entered upon me and was angry. So I said: What has made you angry? He said: By Allaah, I do not recognise anything from the *Ummah* of Muhammad (ﷺ) except that they pray in congregation."[54]

Al-Haafidh Ibn Hajr said in *Fathul-Baaree*: "What Abud-Dardaa meant was that the actions of the people had all suffered deterioration and alteration, except for the fact that they still gathered for congregational Prayer. This is, also a relative matter since the state of the people in the time of Prophethood was more perfect than any period which followed. Then in the time of the two Shaikhs [Aboo Bakr and 'Umar) it was more complete than the period after them. Then this statement came from Abud-Dardaa at the end of his life, towards the end of the *Khilaafah* of 'Uthmaan. So what is our state of affairs today when that was the view of Abud-Dardaa about that excellent time?"

---

[52] Reported by al-Bukhaaree (Eng. trans. 1/350/no.617), Maalik and an-Nasaa'ee from Aboo Hurairah *radiyallaahu 'anhu*.

[53] Reported by al-Bukhaaree (Eng. trans. 1/351/no.618).

[54] Reported by al-Bukhaaree (Eng. trans. 1/353/no.623).

Then alas for us since al-Haafidh Ibn Hajr said that about his time. Then what are we to say about this time when Islaam is a stranger? We find the people have neglected *Jumu'ah* Prayer, congregational Prayers and even Prayer itself?!

So give due importance, O Muslim brother, and be devoted to the congregational Prayer and do not forget his (ﷺ) saying: *For indeed the wolf devours the lone sheep*. Know that Satan watches and waits for you to be distanced from the congregation so that you may come to grief through missing it. Indeed he desires that you abandon the Prayer and Islaam altogether.

Furthermore the mosque is the means for the brothers and those who love one another for Allaah's sake to become acquainted with each other and to strengthen the bonds of love between them, without which *eemaan* will not be easily achieved, this is because there is no easy way to *eemaan*, nor to Paradise except through love for the sake of Allaah, the Most High. Listen, if you wish, to his (ﷺ) saying: *By Him in Whose Hand is my soul, you will not enter Paradise until you have eemaan, and you will not have eemaan until you love one another. Shall I not guide you to something which if you do it you will love one another? Spread the greeting of Salaam amongst yourselves.*[55]

---

[55] Reported by Muslim (Eng. trans. 1/37/no.96) and others.
Publisher's note: The reader is reccomended to refer to *Love and Hate for the Sake of Allaah* by Shaykh Saleem al-Hilaalee (Al-Hidaayah Publishing and Distribution, 1995) for a more detailed discussion on this subject.

2. The Excellence of the Prayer and its Wiping away of Sins and Evil Deeds[56]

From Aboo Hurairah *radiyallaahu 'anhu*, who said that I heard Allaah's Messenger (ﷺ) say: *Do you think that if there was a river at the door of one of you and he bathed in it five times a day, would any dirt remain upon him? They said: No dirt would remain upon him. He said: That is how it is with the five daily Prayers, through them Allaah washes away the sins.*[57]

Aboo Hurairah *radiyallaahu 'anhu*, also narrates, that Allaah's Messenger (ﷺ) said: *The five daily Prayers, and the Jumu'ah to the Jumu'ah are an expiation for what is between them, as long as one is not guilty of major-sins.*[58]

From Aboo Sa'eed al-Khudree *radiyallaahu 'anhu*, that he heard the Prophet (ﷺ) say: *The five daily Prayers are an expiation for whatever is between them. Then Allaah's Messenger (ﷺ) said: Do you see if a man were employed to work and there was between his house and his place of work five rivers. So he comes to his work-place and works as Allaah wills, and becomes dirty or sweaty. Then whenever he came to the river he bathed. What would remain of the dirt? So likewise with the Prayer, whenever he commits a sin he supplicates and seeks forgiveness, so whatever came before is forgiven for him.*[59]

---

[56] All the *ahaadeeth* relating to this chapter are taken from the book *Saheehut-Targheeb wat-Tarheeb*, "Chapter: The excellence of the five daily Prayers and their continual observance," except for the final *hadeeth*.

[57] Reported by al-Bukhaaree (Eng. trans. 1/301/no.506), and Muslim (Eng. trans. 1/324/no.1410), at-Tirmidhee and an-Nasaa'ee.

[58] Reported by Muslim (Eng. trans. 1/151/no.448) and others.

[59] Reported by al-Bazzaar, at-Tabaraanee in *al-Awsat* and *al-Kabeer* with a chain of narration that is satisfactory.

From 'Abdullaah ibn Mas'ood *radiyallaahu 'anhu*, who said that Allaah's Messenger (ﷺ) said: *You fall into destruction,*[60] *you fall into destruction, then when you pray the morning (Subh) Prayer you wash that away. Then you fall into destruction, you fall into destruction, then when you pray the Dhuhr Prayer it washes it away. Then you fall into destruction, you fall into destruction, then when you pray the 'Asr Prayer it washes it away. Then you fall into destruction, you fall into destruction, then when you pray the Maghrib Prayer it washes it away. Then you fall into destruction, you fall into destruction, then when you pray the 'Ishaa Prayer it washes it away. Then you sleep, so nothing is written against you until you awaken.*[61]

From Anas ibn Maalik *radiyallaahu 'anhu*, who said that Allaah's Messenger (ﷺ) said: *Indeed there is for Allaah an angel who proclaims at every Prayer: O children of Aadam! Stand up to the fire which you have ignited and extinguish it.*[62]

From 'Abdullaah ibn Mas'ood *radiyallaahu 'anhu*, who said that Allaah's Messenger (ﷺ) said: *A caller is sent when it is time for each of the Prayers, so he says: 'O children of Aadam, stand up and extinguish what each of you has ignited for themselves,' so their sins fall away from their eyes, and they pray, and they are forgiven what is between them. Then you build up the fire in between them so when it is the first Prayer the call is made: 'O children of Aadam! stand up and extinguish what each of you has ignited for yourselves.' So they stand, purify themselves and pray the Dhuhr Prayer, so they are forgiven whatever was between the two*

---

[60] i.e. by committing many sins.

[61] Reported by at-Tabaraanee in *as-Sagheer* and its narrators are used as proof in the *Saheeh*.

[62] Reported by at-Tabaraanee in *al-Awsat* and *al-Kabeer*.

(Prayers). Then when it is time for the 'Asr Prayer, then the same as that. Then when it is time for Maghrib, then the same as that. Then when it is time for the 'Atamah (i.e. 'Ishaa), then the same as that. Then they sleep having been forgiven, so there are some who spend the night doing good and others who spend it doing evil.[63]

From Taariq ibn Shihaab: That he spent the night in the company of Salmaan al-Farisee *radiyallaahu 'anhu*, in order to observe his worship. He said: So he stood up to pray at the end of the night, and it is as if he did not see what he had expected, so he mentioned that to him, so Salmaan said: "Observe the five daily Prayers, since they are an expiation for these misdeeds as long as he does not fall into that which is a mortal sin."[64]

From 'Amr ibn Murrah al-Juhanee *radiyallaahu 'anhu*, who said: *A man came to the Prophet (ﷺ) and said: O Messenger of Allaah. If I testify that none has the right to be worshipped except Allaah, and that you are the Messenger of Allaah, and I pray the five daily Prayers, and give the Zakaat, and fast and pray (at night) in Ramadaan, then whom will I be from? He said: You will be from the sincere truthful ones, and the martyrs.*[65]

From Aboo 'Uthmaan who said that I was with Salmaan *radiyallaahu 'anhu*, beneath a tree. He took a dried twig from the tree and shook it until its leaves fell off. Then he said: O Aboo 'Uthmaan will you not ask me why I did this? I said: And why did you do it? He said: Allaah's Messenger (ﷺ) did the same with me whilst I was with him beneath a tree. He

---

[63] Reported by at-Tabaraanee in *al-Kabeer*.

[64] Narrated by at-Tabaraanee in *al-Kabeer* as his saying only with a chain of narration which is satisfactory.

[65] Reported by al-Bazzaar, Ibn Khuzaimah and Ibn Hibbaan, and the wording is that of Ibn Hibbaan.

took a dried twig from the tree and shook it until its leaves fell off, then said: *O Salmaan! Will you not ask me why I did this? I said: And why did you do it? He said: When the Muslim makes wudoo and does it well, then he prays the five daily Prayers his sins fall away just as these leaves fall away, and he said:*

وَأَقِمِ ٱلصَّلَوٰةَ طَرَفَيِ ٱلنَّهَارِ وَزُلَفًا مِّنَ
ٱلَّيۡلِۚ إِنَّ ٱلۡحَسَنَٰتِ يُذۡهِبۡنَ ٱلسَّيِّـَٔاتِۚ ذَٰلِكَ ذِكۡرَىٰ لِلذَّٰكِرِينَ

> **"And offer Prayers perfectly, at the two ends of the day and in some hours of the night. Verily, good deeds remove evil deeds. That is a reminder for the mindful."** [66, 67]

From 'Uthmaan *radiyallaahu 'anhu*, who said that Allaah's Messenger (ﷺ) said: *There is no Muslim upon whom the obligatory Prayer becomes due, so he perfects the wudoo, humility and attentiveness (khushoo') and the bowing (rukoo'), except that it is an expiation for the sins coming before it as long as he does not commit a major sin. This applies all the time.* [68]

---

[66] Soorah Hood (11):114

[67] Reported by Ahmad, an-Nasaa'ee and at-Tabaraanee. The reason for the sending down of this *Aayah* is what is reported by al-Bukhaaree (Eng. trans. 6/171-172/no.209) from Ibn Mas'ood *radiyallaahu 'anhu*: A man kissed a woman and then came to Allaah's Messenger (ﷺ) and mentioned that to him, so (the *Aayah*) was revealed. So the man said: Is this for me alone: He (ﷺ) said: *It is for all those from my Ummah who act similarly.*

[68] Reported by Muslim (Eng. trans. 1/150/no.441).

From Aboo Ayyoob *radiyallaahu 'anhu*, that the Prophet (ﷺ) used to say: *Indeed every Prayer removes the sins that come before it.*[69]

From Sa'd ibn Abee Waqqaas who said: There were two men who were brothers and one of them died forty nights before the second. So I mentioned the excellence of the first in the presence of Allaah's Messenger (ﷺ), so Allaah's Messenger (ﷺ) said: *Was not the other one a Muslim? Then I said: Indeed yes and there was nothing wrong with him. So Allaah's Messenger (ﷺ) said: How would you know what (high station) his Prayer has bought him to? Indeed the Prayer is like a river of sweet and abundant water, outside the door of one of you, into which he plunges five times every day. So what dirt do you think would remain upon him? Indeed you do not know the (high station) that his Prayer brought him to.* [70]

From Aboo Hurairah *radiyallaahu 'anhu*, who said: *There were two men from Baliyy, from the (tribe of) Qudaa'ah who accepted Islaam and joined Allaah's Messenger (ﷺ). Then one of then was martyred and the other one died a year later. So Talhah ibn 'Ubaydillaah said: I saw the one delayed (in a dream) and he was entered into Paradise before the martyr, so I was surprised at that. So I mentioned that to Allaah's Messenger (ﷺ), or it was mentioned to Allaah's Messenger (ﷺ), so Allaah's Messenger (ﷺ) said: Did he not fast Ramadaan after him, and pray six-thousand (more) rak'ahs, and such and such Sunnah Prayers.*[71] In an authentic addition reported by Ibn Hibbaan: *Between these two there is a distance greater than what is between the heavens and the earth.*

---

[69] Reported by Ahmad with *hasan* chain of narration.

[70] Reported by Maalik and the wording is his, and Ahmad with a *hasan* chain of narration, and an-Nasaa'ee.

[71] Reported by Ahmad with a *hasan* chain of narration.

From Ibn 'Umar *radiyallaahu 'anhu*, who said that Allaah's Messenger (ﷺ) said: *When the worshipper stands up in Prayer all his sins are brought and placed upon his head and shoulders. So whenever he bows and prostrates they fall from him.*[72]

From Thawbaan *radiyallaahu 'anhu*, who said that Allaah's Messenger (ﷺ) said: *Remain upon the straight way, which you will not be able to do fully (except with Allaah's help), and know that the best of your actions is the Prayer, and no one gives care and attention to the wudoo except a Believer.*[73]

From Aboo Maalik al-Ash'aree *radiyallaahu 'anhu*, who said that Allaah's Messenger (ﷺ) said: *Purification is half of eemaan, 'al-hamdu lillaah' (All praise and thanks are for Allaah) fills the Balance (al-Meezaan), and 'subhaanallaah' (Allaah is free and far removed from all imperfections) and 'al-hamdu lillaah' fill whatever is between the heavens and the earth. The Prayer is light, charity (sadaqah) is a clear proof, patient endurance (sabr) is a shining light, and the Qur'aan is a proof for you or against you.*[74]

From Aboo Dharr *radiyallaahu 'anhu*, that the Prophet (ﷺ) went out in winter and the leaves were falling. So he took hold of the branch of a tree and the leaves began falling off, then he said: *O Aboo Dharr. I said: At your service O Messenger of Allaah! He said: Indeed the Muslim serv-*

---

[72] Reported by at-Tabaraanee in *al-Kabeer* and al-Baihaqee in *as-Sunan* and it is found in *Saheehul-Jaami'* (no.1671).

[73] Reported by al-Haakim who declared it *saheeh* to the standard of al-Bukhaaree and Muslim. It has no point of weakness except a mistake of Aboo Bilaal, and Ibn Hibbaan reports its like in his *Saheeh* through a narrator other than Aboo Bilaal. It occurs in *Saheehut-Targheeb* (no.375).

[74] Reported by Muslim (Eng. trans. 1/147/no.432) and others.

ant prays the Prayer, seeking Allaah's Face by it, and his sins fall away just as the leaves fall away from this tree.[75]

From Rabee'ah ibn Ka'b who said that I used to spend the night along with Allaah's Messenger (ﷺ) and I would bring him water for *wudoo* and whatever he needed. So he said to me: *Ask me. So I said: I ask only for your companionship in Paradise. He said: Do you wish to ask for something else? I said: That is it. He said: Then assist me with regard to your soul by making much prostration.*[76]

From Aboo Hurairah *radiyallaahu 'anhu*, who said that Allaah's Messenger (ﷺ) said: *The Prayer is the best of what has been prescribed, so he who is able to perform a great deal of it then let him do so.*[77]

From Aboo Hurairah *radiyallaahu 'anhu*, that Allaah's Messenger (ﷺ) passed by a grave and said: *Who is the occupant of this grave? They said: So and so. He said: Two rak'ahs would be more beloved to him then the rest of your world.*[78]

Points of benefit that can be taken from these *ahaadeeth*:

(1) That Allaah, the Most High, wipes away sins through the five daily Prayers.

---

[75] Reported by Ahmad with *hasan* chain of narration.

[76] Reported by Muslim (Eng. trans. 1/256/no.990).

[77] Reported by at-Tabaraanee in *al-Awsat*. Shaikh al-Albaanee said: "It has supports which strengthen it, since it is reported by at-Tayaalisee, Ahmad and al-Haakim through two chains of narration from Aboo Dharr. It is also reported by Ahmad and others from the *hadeeth* of Aboo Umaamah, so the *hadeeth* is *hasan* if Allaah wills."

[78] Reported by at-Tabaraanee in *al-Awsat* with *hasan* chain of narration.

(2) That the Prayer is an expiation of what is committed between them, as long as major sins are avoided.

(3) Sins destroy a person and ignite a fire for him which he must extinguish with the Prayers.

(4) The Muslim may reach the station of the sincere, the truthful, and the martyrs through Prayer, *Zakaat* and Fasting.

(5) The excellence of Prayer over other actions.[79]

(6) That Allaah, the Most High, blessed that Companion by entering him into Paradise before his brother, the martyr, and that was because he had performed more Prayers than him.

(7) That Prayer is a light which will make the way clear for the servant in this life and the Hereafter.

(8) That the way to achieve companionship of the Prophet (ﷺ) in Paradise is to increase in performance of prostration and Prayer.

(9) That performance of two *rak'ahs* would be more beloved to a deceased person than the world and all that it contains.

(10) That turning with ones heart to Allaah in the Prayer fully and sincerely causes the Muslim to be as he was on the day his mother gave birth to him [i.e. free from sin].

---

[79] With the condition that the *'aqeedah* (creed) of the person is correct and free from corruption.

3. The Effect of the Prayer in the Abandonment of Sins and in Purifying and Developing the Soul

Allaah, the One free and far removed from all defects, says:

إِنَّ ٱلصَّلَوٰةَ تَنْهَىٰ عَنِ ٱلْفَحْشَآءِ وَٱلْمُنكَرِ

> **"Verily, Prayer prevents one from shameful and evil deeds."**[80]

So Allaah, the Most High, explains in this *Aayah* that the Prayer done with humility and attentiveness, and performed correctly must certainly lead the person away from wickedness and evil actions, and lead him to doing good. Therefore you will find those who pray in the mosques are the best of the people, despite any faults they may have, and any faults they do have or sins they commit, then this will be found to a far greater degree in others.

However if the Prayer does not prevent us from wickedness and evil actions then we must carefully examine what is going wrong and how to correct it. Indeed the Prayer must be rectified and prayed with full humility and attentiveness. So let us look closely at the causes and strive to find the cure. Just as we seek to treat our bodies from illness, then it is even more appropriate that we should seek to find the cure for our souls. This will help us to understand the saying of the Prophet (ﷺ): *The first thing for which the person will be accountable on the Day of Resurrection is the Prayer. So if it is in order, then the rest of his actions will be in order. But if it is defective then the rest of his actions will be defective.*[81]

---

[80] Soorah al-'Ankaboot (29):45

[81] Reported by at-Tabaraanee in *al-Awsat* and *ad-Diyaa*, from Anas *radiyallaahu 'anhu*, and it is found in *Saheebul-Jaami'* (no.2570).

If the Prayer is corrected then the rest of the actions will be corrected, since it is like the head with regard to the rest of the body. Furthermore, the closest that a servant is to his Lord is when he is in Prayer, calling upon his Lord, seeking His forgiveness, turning to Him and weeping before Him. Then the Prayer cannot be corrected unless one's *'aqeedah* (creed and belief) is corrected, and what that comprehends: being mindful of Allaah, the Most High, and fearing Him, and remembering that one will have to stand before Him for the Reckoning, and being terrified of His Fire. So that when he is tempted to commit sins he finds in his heart the ability to repel and reject them, since he looks at the present and temporary pleasure, and at the bliss which never ends and the happiness which never ceases, and he prefers the lasting good to that which will perish and pass away.

The Prayer of a person is ruined by his failing to be mindful of Allaah, the Most High, and by weakness of *taqwaa,*[82] thus this person does not have such fear as will prevent him from committing sins. As occurs in the *hadeeth*: *...Indeed there is in the body a piece flesh which if it is sound then the whole body is sound, and if it is corrupt then the whole body is corrupt. Indeed it is the heart.*[83]

This asserts that the soundness of the whole body depends on the soundness of the heart, and if the heart is corrupt then the whole body shall be corrupt. If the heart is sound then the hand shall be sound and shall not steal, nor reach for that which is forbidden nor commit fornication by the forbidden touch. The feet also shall be sound and so shall not walk to that which is forbidden. The ear shall be sound and so shall not listen to

---

[82] Translator's note: *Taqwaa* meaning acting in obedience to Allaah by doing what He has ordered and avoiding what He has forbidden.

[83] Reported by al-Bukhaaree (Eng. trans. 1/44/no.49) and Muslim (Eng. trans. 3/840/no.3882) from the *hadeeth* of an-Nu'maan ibn Basheer *radiyallaahu 'anhu*.

music, to tale carrying, nor to backbiting. The tongue shall be in good condition and shall not speak except good. But if the heart is corrupt then it shall not lead the rest of the body except in corruption.

The heart will be rectified or corrupted through the Prayer, so if the Prayer is perfect and correct then this shows that the heart is benefiting and is sound, but if not then it indicates that it is not benefiting properly and that it is corrupted, so that it manifests evil which covers the rest of the body.

Know that each Prayer that is prayed with humility and attentiveness incites the heart towards righteous actions and good deeds, just as every good deed outside the Prayer increases ones humility and attentiveness in it. There occurs in the *hadeeth*: *Perform the Night Prayer (Qiyaamul-Layl), since it was the practice of the pious before you, and draws one near to Allaah, the Most High, and is a prevention of evil deeds, and an expiation of sins.*[84]

So the Prophet (ﷺ) made clear that the Night Prayer (*Qiyaamul-Layl*) is a prevention of evil deeds, since it forbids a person from sin and evil and commands him to good. So we must observe and increase in Prayer, and must observe the Night Prayer. Standing fearfully and humbly before Allaah, the One free and far removed of all defects, weeping from our hearts due to our failings and shortcomings, and hoping for the mercy of our Lord, the Most High, supplicating Him that He should make us firm upon the truth, and to make our Prayer and our standing at night of benefit to us.

---

[84] Reported by Ahmad, at-Tirmidhee and others and it is found in *Saheehul-Jaami'* (no.3958).

It was said to the Prophet (ﷺ): *So and so prays all the night, but in the daytime he steals! So he replied: What you say will prevent him, or he said: His Prayer will prevent him.*[85]

If the servant's Prayer reaches its required level as prevention from sins, then it will be written for the person in the register of righteous deeds in the seventh heaven (*'Illiyyoon*) as occurs in the *hadeeth*: *Prayer followed by Prayer with no idle talk between them is recorded in 'Illiyyoon.*[86]

Also do not forget that the Prayer is a means of preventing you from entering upon evil or going out to it due to what Aboo Hurairah *radiyallaahu 'anhu*, reports from the Prophet (ﷺ) that he said: *When one of you is going to leave his house then let him pray two rak'ahs, they will prevent you going out to evil, and when you enter your house then pray two rak'ahs, they will prevent you from entering upon evil.*[87]

---

[85] Reported by Ahmad, al-Bazzaar and others and declared *saheeh* by our Shaikh [al-Albaanee] in *Silsilatul-Ahaadeethid-Da'eefah* (1/16).

[86] Reported by Aboo Daawood (Eng. trans. 1/338/no.1283) and is found in *Saheehul-Jaami'* (no.3731).

[87] Reported by al-Bazzaar and al-Baihaqee in *Shu'abul-Eemaan* and it is found in *Saheehul-Jaami'* (no.518).

4. Perfecting the Prayer, Having Humility and Attentiveness (*Khushoo'*) in it, and the Reward for that

From 'Uqbah ibn'Aamir *radiyallaahu 'anhu*, who said that Allaah's Messenger (ﷺ) said: *There is no one who makes wudoo and makes it well, and prays two rak'ahs being fully attentive with his heart and his face in them, except that Paradise is obligatory for him.*[88]

From Zayd ibn Khaalid al-Juhanee *radiyallaahu 'anhu*, that Allaah's Messenger (ﷺ) said: *Whoever makes wudoo and makes it well, and then prays two rak'ahs, not being unmindful in them, then his previous sins are forgiven.*[89]

From Humraan, the freed slave of 'Uthmaan *radiyallaahu 'anhu*, that he witnessed 'Uthmaan ibn 'Affaan *radiyallaahu 'anhu*, call for water for *wudoo*. Then poured water from the jug over his hands and washed them three times. Then he entered his right hand into the water and then washed his mouth and washed his nose and blew the water out. Then he washed his face three times, and washed his arms up to and including the elbows three times. Then he wiped his head. Then he washed his feet three times. Then he said: *I saw Allaah's Messenger (ﷺ) making wudoo, like this wudoo of mine, then he (ﷺ) said: Whoever performs wudoo like the wudoo of mine, and then prays two rak'ahs in which he does not allow his the mind to wander, then his previous sins are forgiven.*[90]

---

[88] Reported by Muslim (Eng. trans. 1/152/no.451).

[89] Reported by Aboo Daawood (Eng. trans. 1/230/no.904) and it is found in *Saheehut-Targheeb* (no.223).

[90] Reported by al-Bukhaaree (Eng. trans. 1/113/161) and Muslim (Eng. trans. 1/149/no.436).

From Aboo Dardaa *radiyallaahu 'anhu*, who said that I heard Allaah's Messenger (ﷺ) saying: *Whoever makes wudoo and makes it well, then he stands and prays two rak'ahs, or four,* (Sahl the subnarrator was doubtful about which), *perfecting the remembrance (of Allaah) and the humility and the attentiveness (khushoo') in them, and then asks Allaah's forgiveness, then he is forgiven.*[91]

At the end of the *hadeeth* of 'Amr ibn 'Abasah *radiyallaahu 'anhu*, there occurs: *...So if he stands and prays, and praises Allaah, exalts Him and glorifies Him with what befits Him, and turns with all his heart to Allaah, the Most High, then his sins would leave him until he is just as he was on the day on which his mother gave birth to him.*[92]

From Jaabir *radiyallaahu 'anhu*, who said that I asked Allaah's Messenger (ﷺ) about brushing away small pebbles whilst praying, so he said: *Once, but if you refrain from that then it is better for you than one hundred camels, all of them having black eyes.*[93]

---

[91] Reported by Ahmad with *hasan* chain of narration, as occurs in *Saheehut-Targheeb* (no.392).

[92] Reported by Muslim (Eng. trans. 2/395-397/no.1812).

[93] Reported by Ibn Khuzaimah in his *saheeh* and it occurs in *Saheehut-Targheeb* (no.558).

5. The Excellence of the Night Prayer (*Qiyaamul-Layl*) and its Effect in increasing *Eemaan* [94]

If the Muslim carefully considered *Sooratul-Muzammil* he would find the greatest lesson in it, since Allaah, the One free and far removed from all defects and the Most High, ordered the Messenger of Allaah (ﷺ) to establish the Night Prayer (*Qiyaamul-Layl*) when he was in a very difficult situation, and he (ﷺ) was in the direst need of help and assistance. So there is in the saying of Allaah, the Most High,

يَٰٓأَيُّهَا ٱلْمُزَّمِّلُ ﴿١﴾ قُمِ ٱلَّيْلَ إِلَّا قَلِيلًا ﴿٢﴾

> **"O you wrapped in garments (i.e. Prophet Muhammad (ﷺ))! Stand to pray all night, except a little."**[95]

Cultivation and training for the soul, and refinement and reassurance for the heart of the Prophet (ﷺ). The Night Prayer used to be an obligation upon the Prophet (ﷺ) and his Companions *radiyallaahu 'anhum*, as occurs in *Saheeh Muslim* in a long *hadeeth* from Zuraarah *radiyallaahu 'anhu*, and in it there occurs: ... she [i.e. 'Aa'ishah] said: "Do you [i.e. Sa'd ibn Hishaam] not recite:

يَٰٓأَيُّهَا ٱلْمُزَّمِّلُ ﴿١﴾

"O you wrapped in garments (i.e. Prophet Muhammad (ﷺ))!" ?"

I said: "Indeed yes." She said: "Then Allaah, the Mighty and Majestic, obligated the Night Prayer at the beginning of this *Soorah*. So the Prophet (ﷺ) and his Companions observed it for a year, and Allaah withheld the

---

[94] All these *ahaadeeth* are taken from *Saheehut-Targheeb wat-Tarheeb*.

[95] Soorah al-Muzammil (73):1-2.

end of it for twelve months in the heavens, until Allaah sent down the conclusion of the *Soorah* when the duty was eased and the Night Prayer became optional after having been an obligation."[96]

So indeed there must be hidden benefits arising from the Night Prayer. Indeed it is a preparation for men. It makes the hearts firm upon the truth, and further strengthens them. It is the secret of success. It distances a person from sins and evil actions. It increases *eemaan*. It causes a person to be joined with the righteous and raises him to the level of the sincere worshippers, and those who worship Him as if they are seeing Him, even though they do not see Him, yet He, the Most High, certainly sees them.

From Aboo Hurairah *radiyallaahu 'anhu*, that Allaah's Messenger (ﷺ) said: *Satan ties three knots*[97] *at the back of the head of one of you when he sleeps, sealing every knot with: 'The night is long so remain asleep.' Then when one of you awakes and remembers Allaah, the Most High, one knot is undone. When one makes wudoo a knot is undone, and*

---

[96] Reported by Muslim (Eng. trans. 1/358-361/no.1623).

[97] Shaikh al-Albaanee *hafidhahullaah*, says in *Saheehut-Targheeb*: "There are various sayings about the meaning of 'knots' (*al-'uqad*) and the most correct is that it is meant literally, and is a form of magic practised upon the person to prevent him from getting up to pray, just as sorcerers use knots, as He the Patron and Protector informed in His Book:

وَمِن شَرِّ ٱلنَّفَّٰثَٰتِ فِى ٱلْعُقَدِ ٤

"And from the evil of witchcrafts when they blow in the knots."

[Soorah al-Falaq (113):4]

So the unfortunate is the one whom he is able to get the better of, and the one saved is the one whom he is prevented from. A further proof that it is meant literally is what Ibn Maajah reports from Aboo Hurairah *radiyallaahu 'anhu*, from the Prophet (ﷺ): *Upon the back of the head of you is a rope with three knots...* Also what Ibn Khuzaimah reports, and the author mentions it in this chapter from Jaabir *radiyallaahu 'anhu*: *Upon his head is knotted rope*."

when one prays all the knots are undone so he wakes energetic and in good spirits. But if not then he wakes in bad spirits and is sluggish.[98]

In a narration:[99] *So he awakes energetic, in good spirits, having attained good. But if he does not do so, then he awakes sluggish, in bad spirits, not having attained good.*

From Jaabir *radiyallaahu 'anhu*, who said that Allaah's Messenger (ﷺ) said: *There is no male or female except that upon their head is a rope which is knotted when they sleep at night. So if he wakes and remembers Allaah a knot is untied. Then if he makes wudoo and prays the knots are (all) untied and he awakens light and in good spirits having attained good.*[100]

From Aboo Hurairah *radiyallaahu 'anhu*, that Allaah's Messenger (ﷺ) said: *The best fast after Ramadaan is in Allaah's month of Muharram, and the best Prayer after the obligatory Prayer is the Night Prayer (Salaatul-Layl).*[101]

From 'Abdullaah ibn 'Umar *radiyallaahu 'anhu*, who said that Allaah's Messenger (ﷺ) said: *In Paradise there is a (raised) chamber the outside of which can be seen from its inside, and whose inside can be seen from its outside. So Aboo Maalik al-Ash'aree said: "Who is it for O Messenger of Allaah?" He said: For those whose speech is good, who provide*

---

[98] Reported by al-Bukhaaree (Eng. trans. 2/134/no.243) and Muslim (Eng. trans. 1/376/no.1702).

[99] Of Ibn Maajah.

[100] Reported by Ibn Khuzaimah in his *Saheeh*.

[101] Reported by Muslim (Eng. trans. 2/269/2611), Aboo Daawood (Eng. trans. 2/668/2423), at-Tirmidhee, an-Nasaa'ee, and Ibn Khuzaimah in his *Saheeh*.

with food, and who stand the night (in Prayer) whilst the people are sleeping.[102]

From al-Mugheerah ibn Shu'bah *radiyallaahu 'anhu*, who said: *The Prophet (ﷺ) stood in Prayer until his feet swelled up. So it was said to him: Allaah has forgiven your earlier and later sins. He replied: Should I not be a thankful servant.*[103]

From 'Abdullaah ibn 'Amr ibn al-'Aas *radiyallaahu 'anhu*, who said that I heard Allaah's Messenger (ﷺ) say: *The most beloved of Prayers to Allaah is the Prayer of Daawood and the most beloved of Fasts to Allaah is the Fast of Daawood. He used to sleep for half of the night, stand (in Prayer) for a third of it and sleep for a sixth of it. He used to fast one day and refrain from fasting the (next) day.*[104]

From Jaabir *radiyallaahu 'anhu*, who said that I heard Allaah's Messenger (ﷺ) say: *Indeed in the night there is an hour which no Muslim man encounters whilst asking Allaah for the good of this world and the Hereafter except that He gives it to him, and that is every night.*[105]

From Aboo Umaamah al-Baahilee *radiyallaahu 'anhu*, that Allaah's Messenger (ﷺ) said: *Perform the Night Prayer, for it was the practice of the*

---

[102] Reported by at-Tabaraanee in *al-Kabeer* with a *hasan* chain of narration, and al-Haakim who declared it *saheeh* to the standard of al-Bukhaaree and Muslim.

[103] Reported by al-Bukhaaree (Eng. trans. 2/128/no.130) and Muslim (Eng. trans. 4/1474/no.6772).

[104] Reported by al-Bukhaaree (Eng. trans. 2/129/no.231) and Muslim (Eng. trans. 2/565/no.2595).

[105] Reported by Muslim (Eng. trans. 1/365/no.1654).

pious before you, and draws one near to Allaah, the Most High and is an expiation of sins and a prevention of evil deeds.[106]

From Aboo Hurairah *radiyallaahu 'anhu*, who said that Allaah's Messenger (ﷺ) said: *May Allaah have mercy upon the man who gets up at night and prays, and awakens his wife, and if she refuses then he sprinkles water upon her face, and may Allaah have mercy upon a woman who gets up at night and prays, and awakens her husband, and if he refuses then she sprinkles water upon his face.*[107]

From Aboo Hurairah and Aboo Sa'eed *radiyallaahu 'anhumaa*, who both said that Allaah's Messenger (ﷺ) said: *If a man wakes his wife at night and they both pray, or they pray two rak'ahs together, then they are written amongst those men and women who remember Allaah.*[108]

From Aboo-Dardaa *radiyallaahu 'anhu*, from the Prophet (ﷺ) that he said: *There are three whom Allaah loves, and on account of whom He laughs109 and is delighted: The one who when his companions are overcome fights after them by himself for Allaah, the Mighty and Majestic, and is either killed or granted victory and protected by Allaah. So He says: 'Look at this servant of Mine, how he made himself stand firm for Me.' The one who has a beautiful wife and a soft bed, yet he stands in Prayer during the night, so He says: 'He leaves his desires and remembers Me, and if he had wished he would have slept.' The one who is on a journey along with companions. So they enter upon the night and sleep whereas he stands in Prayer in the hours before daybreak, whether in*

---

[106] Reported by Ahmad, at-Tirmidhee and others and found in *Saheehul-Jaami'* (no.3958).

[107] Reported by Aboo Daawood (Eng. trans. 1/344/no.1303), an-Nasaa'ee, Ibn Maajah and others.

[108] Reported by Aboo Daawood (Eng. trans. 1/344/no.1304), an-Nasaa'ee, Ibn Maajah and others.

difficult circumstances or in ease.[110]

From Ibn Mas'ood *radiyallaahu 'anhu*, from the Prophet (ﷺ) who said: *Our Lord is delighted with two men: A man who gets up from his bedding and his cover, his family and his beloved in order to pray. So Allaah, the Majestic and Most High, says: 'O My angels look at My servant who has got up from his bedding and his cover, his family and his beloved in order to pray out of desire for what there is with Me, and out of fear of what there is with Me.' Also the man who fights in the path of Allaah and his companions are defeated and he knows what responsibility there will be upon him for defeat and he knows what there is for him in returning. So he returns until his blood is shed, so Allaah says to His angels: 'Look at My servant he returned hoping for what there is with Me, and fearing what there is with Me, until his blood was shed.'*[111]

In a narration reported only as the words of Ibn Mas'ood *radiyallaahu 'anhu*:[112] *Indeed Allaah laughs for two men: A man who gets up on a cold night from his bed, his blanket and his cover and makes wudoo, and then stands to pray. Allaah, the Mighty and Majestic, says to His Angels: 'What has lead My servant to do what he has done?' So they say: 'Our Lord, hoping for what there is with You, and fearing what there is*

---

[109] A laughter which befits His Majesty, He the One free and far removed from all imperfections, about which it is not to be said: 'How?' nor is any resemblance to be made with the creation, and likewise with regard to his (ﷺ) saying: "*Our Lord is delighted...*" which follows.

[110] Reported by at-Tabaraanee in *al-Kabeer* with *hasan* chain of narration.

[111] Reported by Ahmad, Aboo Ya'laa and others.

[112] However it has the ruling of being the words of the Prophet (ﷺ) since it is not possible to speak about matters of the unseen (*al-Ghayb*) with ones opinion.

with You.' So He says: 'Then I have given him what he hoped for and have saved him from what he fears...'[113]

From 'Uqbah ibn 'Aamir *radiyallaahu 'anhu*, who said that I heard Allaah's Messenger (ﷺ) say: *A man of my Ummah gets up at night, strives against his own self to purify himself and there are knots upon him, so when he washes his hands a knot is untied, when he washes his face a knot is untied, when he wipes his head a knot is untied and when he washes his feet a knot is untied. So Allaah, the Mighty and Majestic, says to those who are behind the screen: 'Look at this servant of Mine striving against his own self making request to Me. Whatever this servant of Mine asks Me then it is his.*[114]

From 'Abdullaah ibn 'Umar *radiyallaahu 'anhumaa*, who said that Allaah's Messenger (ﷺ) said: *There is to be no envy*[115] *except with regard to two: A man to whom Allaah has granted the Qur'aan, so that he stands in Prayer reading it throughout the night and day; and a man whom Allaah has given wealth and who gives it in charity day and night.*[116]

From Fadaalah ibn 'Ubayd and Tameem ad-Daaree, *radiyallaahu 'anhumaa*, from the Prophet (ﷺ) that he said: *Whoever stands up (in Prayer) with ten Aayaat in a night will have a huge amount (Qintaar) of reward written for him, and this amount is better than the world and whatever it contains. So when it is the Day of Resurrection your Lord,*

---

[113] Reported by at-Tabaraanee with *hasan* chain of narration see *Saheehut-Targheeb* (no.626).

[114] Reported by Ahmad and Ibn Hibbaan in his *Saheeh* and the wording is his.

[115] Envy here meaning a desire to possess that quality without wishing for it to be taken away from the one already possessing it.

[116] Reported by Muslim (Eng. trans. 2/388/no.1777) and others.

the Mighty and Majestic, will say: "Recite and ascend one rank for every Aayah." Until the last Aayah which he has, then Allaah, the Mighty and Majestic, will say to the servant: "Take hold." So the servant will say with his hand: 'O my Lord! You know better.' He will say: "With this (take hold of) everlasting life, and with this (take hold of) [117] *everlasting bliss".*

From 'Abdullaah ibn 'Amr ibn al-'Aas *radiyallaahu 'anhumaa*, who said that Allaah's Messenger (ﷺ) said: *Whoever stands (in Prayer) with ten Aayaat will not be written amongst the negligent, and whoever stands (in Prayer) with a hundred Aayaat will be written amongst the obedient servants, and whoever stands (in Prayer) with a thousand Aayaat will be written amongst those who receive huge rewards.*[118]

From Aboo Hurairah *radiyallaahu 'anhu*, who said that Allaah's Messenger (ﷺ) said: *Whoever prays at night with a hundred Aayaat will not be written amongst the negligent, and whoever prays at night with two hundred Aayaat will be written amongst the sincere and obedient servants.*[119]

Points of benefit that can be taken from these *ahaadeeth*:

(1) The Prayer has a share in the removal of the knots which Satan ties at the back of the person's head.

---

[117] Translator's note: i.e. with the right hand take hold of everlasting life and with the left hand take hold of everlasting bliss, as shown in a narration of Ibn 'Asaakir see *Saheehut-Targheeb* (no.634).

[118] Reported by Aboo Daawood (Eng. trans. 1/367/no.1393) and Ibn Khuzaimah in his *Saheeh*.

[119] From a narration of Ibn Khuzaimah. Al-Haakim declared it *saheeh* to the standard of Muslim.

(2) Night-Prayer (*Salaatul-Layl*) is the best Prayer after the obligatory Prayers.

(3) The person who stands to pray during the night attains a reward which is not attained by many people.

(4) Expressing thankfulness to Allaah, the Most High, by Prayer and Fasting.

(5) The most beloved of Prayers to Allaah, the Most High, is the Prayer of Daawood: praying for one third of the night and sleeping for two thirds.

(6) That Allaah, the Most High, has blessed His servant with an hour at night when supplication is certainly responded to, so the Muslim should seek after it, and strive to attain it, so that he may receive the good of this life and the Hereafter.

(7) That standing in the Night Prayer is a sign of a person's well-being and piety, it expiates sins and prevents from evil deeds.

(8) That Allaah, the Most High, covers with His Mercy the husband and wife who strive together to perform the Night Prayer. So if one of them refuses the other sprinkles water upon their face.

(9) That standing in Prayer for two *rak'ahs* during the night makes a person one of those men or women who remember Allaah much.

(10) That Allaah, the Most High, is delighted with a man who leaves his bedding and his cover, his family and beloved, and He, the One free and far removed from all defects, laughs due to him, and boasts of him before the angels.

(11) There is to be no envy and no vying except with regard to two: one of them being he who stands in the Night Prayer reciting the Book of Allaah, the Most High.

(12) Whoever recites ten *Aayaat* in a night is not written amongst the negligent and a large reward is written for him, and Allaah, the Most High, will say to him on the Day of Resurrection: 'Recite and ascend one rank for every *Aayah,*' until the final *Aayah* which he has with him, and Allaah, the Most High, will bless him with everlasting life.

(13) Whoever stands with a hundred *Aayaat* is written amongst the obedient servants, and whoever stands with a thousand *Aayaat* is written amongst those who receive huge rewards and whoever stands with two hundred *Aayaat* is written amongst the sincere and obedient servants.

6. The Husband and Wife Encouraging One Another to Perform the Night Prayer

From Aboo Hurairah *radiyallaahu 'anhu*, who said that Allaah's Messenger (ﷺ) said: *May Allaah have mercy upon a man who gets up at night and prays, and awakens his wife, and if she refuses then he sprinkles water on her face, and may Allaah have mercy upon a woman who gets up at night and prays, and awakens her husband, and if he refuses then she sprinkles water upon his face.*[120]

[120] Reported by Aboo Daawood (Eng. trans. 1/344/no.1303), an-Nasaa'ee, Ibn Maajah and others see *Saheehut-Targheeb* (no.621).

7. The Most Beloved Prayer to Allaah

From Ibn 'Amr *radiyallaahu 'anhu*, who said that Allaah's Messenger (ﷺ) said: *The most beloved of Fasting to Allaah is the Fasting of Daawood: he used to fast for a day and refrain from fasting the (next) day, and the most beloved of Prayers to Allaah is the Prayer of Daawood: he used to sleep for half of the night, pray for one third of it, and sleep for one sixth of it.*[121]

---

[121] Reported by al-Bukhaaree (Eng. trans. 4/418/no.631), Muslim (Eng. trans. 2/565/ no.2596), Ahmad and others.

8. Allaah, the Most High, Turns His Face to His Praying Servant

From al-Haarith ibn al-Haarith al-Ash'aree *radiyallaahu 'anhu*, who said that Allaah's Messenger (ﷺ) said: ...*when you stand to pray then do not turn aside, since Allaah, the Mighty and Majestic, turns His Face to His servant as long as he does not turn aside.*[122]

[122] Part of a *hadeeth* reported by al-Bukhaaree in his *Taareekh*, Ahmad in his *Musnad* and others and is found in *Saheehul-Jaami'* (no.1720).

9. Seeking Help Through Prayer

Allaah, the Most High, says:

وَٱسْتَعِينُوا۟ بِٱلصَّبْرِ وَٱلصَّلَوٰةِ ۚ وَإِنَّهَا لَكَبِيرَةٌ إِلَّا عَلَى ٱلْخَٰشِعِينَ ﴿٤٥﴾ ٱلَّذِينَ يَظُنُّونَ أَنَّهُم مُّلَٰقُوا۟ رَبِّهِمْ وَأَنَّهُمْ إِلَيْهِ رَٰجِعُونَ ﴿٤٦﴾

> **"And seek help in patience and Prayer and truly it is heavy except for those who humble themselves (before Allaah)."**[123]

Ibn Katheer says in his *Tafseer*: "Seek help in striving for the Hereafter by persevering in carrying out the obligatory duties and the Prayer." He further says: "...the Prayer is one of the greatest aids to remaining firm."

From Hudhayfah *radiyallaahu 'anhu* who said: "When anything distressed him (the Prophet (ﷺ)) he would pray."[124]

This is the true Prayer by means of which the servant turns for refuge and help to Allaah, the Most High, from all sorrows, distress, grief and anxiety. So he then feels consolation and that he is aided by Allaah, the Most High, the Lord of the heavens and the earth. This assists him to proceed successfully through this life and gain the Pleasure of Allaah, the One free and far removed from all imperfections and the Most High, and he wins Paradise whose width is like the heavens and the earth.

---

[123] Soorah al-Baqarah (2):45-46

[124] Reported by Ahmad in his *Musnad* and Aboo Daawood (Eng. trans. 1/347/1314) and is found in *Saheehul-Jaami'* (no.4579).

Did not the Prophet (ﷺ) say: *The closest that a servant is to his Lord is when he is prostrating, so make much supplication.*[125] So let us seek the assistance of supplication in prostration, and let us earnestly humble ourselves before Allaah, the Most High, and beseech Him to remove our distress and to grant us the good of this world and the Hereafter. The story of that Companion is not far from us, the Companion who asked the Prophet (ﷺ) for his companionship in Paradise. So what advice did he give him? What action did he guide him to? What did he say to him? *"Then assist me with regard to your soul by making much prostration."*[126] So he guided him to make much prostration in order to attain his greatest goal and highest aim.

---

[125] Reported by Muslim (Eng. trans. 1/254/no.979) and others.

[126] The full *hadeeth* is found in the chapter: "The Excellence of the Prayer and that it Wipes away Sins and Evil Deeds."

10. The Connection Between Prayer and the Affairs of Life

The Prayer is not just a form of worship which is meant for the attainment of the Hereafter alone, rather it is closely connected to the life of the Muslim. It prevents him from sins and evil deeds, as has preceded, and affects his behaviour. It is a mirror of his actions, reflecting whether they are in good order or whether they are corrupted.

It has a profound effect upon his trustworthiness in his dealings, and upon his fulfilling what he is entrusted with, causing him to be a good neighbour, to have good manners, to give preference to others and to avoid harming them. So that happiness, harmony and affection are found in the house and the family, in the street and the society, indeed throughout the *Ummah*.

If the Muslim intends to carry out some important matter he performs *Salaatul-Istikhaarah* (Prayer for seeking Allaah's guidance and help), so he prays two *rak'ahs* then supplicates to his Lord to guide him to what is correct, and that He makes easy for him whatever is good for his religion, worldly life and the conclusion of his affairs. This is due to what is established from Jaabir *radiyallaahu 'anhu* who said that Allaah's Messenger (ﷺ) said: *When one of you wishes to carry out some affair then let him pray two rak'ahs, other than the compulsory ones, and then let him say: 'O Allaah I ask you for guidance due to Your knowledge, and I ask for help due to your Power, and I ask from Your great bounty, for indeed You have the ability and I do not have the ability, and You know and I do not know, and You are the knower of the Unseen. O Allaah if You know that this affair* - and he should name it - *is good for me in my religion, my livelihood, and for the conclusion of my affairs, for the present and the future, then ordain it for me and make it easy for me, then bless me in it. But if You know that this matter is bad for me in my religion, my livelihood, and for the conclusion of my affairs, for the present and the future, then turn it away from me and turn me away from it, and ordain for me what is good, wherever it is, and make me pleased with it.*[127]

If there is an eclipse of the sun or the moon the Muslim turns anxiously to his Lord, praying and supplicating until it is removed, since it is Allaah, the Most High, who through it causes His servants to fear. As he (ﷺ) said: *The sun and the moon are not eclipsed due to the death of anyone nor his life, but rather they are signs from the signs of Allaah by which Allaah causes His servants to fear. So when you see that, then pray and supplicate until it is removed from you.*[128] In a narration: *So supplicate to Allaah, declare His greatness, pray and give charity.*[129]

Likewise when a Muslim dies, his brothers and those who have love for him and those who seek reward hasten to carry out what is necessary for their brother, and from this is the Funeral Prayer. In this state the servant is in the direst need of the Mercy of his Lord. So if forty men who do not associate anything in worship with Allaah pray over him then Allaah, the Most High, accepts their intercession for him, and this is due to what Ibn 'Abbaas *radiyallaahu 'anhumaa*, reports from the Prophet (ﷺ) that he said: *There is no Muslim who dies and forty men who do not associate anything in worship with Allaah pray over him, except that Allaah accepts their intercession for him.*[130] In a narration: *There is no one who dies and a company of Muslims whose number reaches a hundred pray*

---

[127] Reported by al-Bukhaaree (Eng. trans. 2/146/no.263) and others.

[128] Reported by al-Bukhaaree, Muslim (Eng. trans. 2/428/no.1972) and others.

[129] Reported by al-Bukhaaree and Muslim (Eng. trans. 2/84/no.154).

[130] Reported by Ahmad, Muslim (Eng. trans. 2/450/no.2072) and others.

over him, and intercede for him, except that their intercession is accepted for him.[131]

Also in the *'Eid* Prayer the people of the town gather together and perform the Prayer, and this provides an opportunity for them to meet and become acquainted with each other, and for them to increase in friendship and love. The Prophet (ﷺ) also used to send out armies for military expeditions from the Prayer-ground. This is what is reported by Aboo Sa'eed al-Khudree *radiyallaahu 'anhu*, who said: "Allaah's Messenger (ﷺ) used to go out on the day of *Fitr* and the day of *Adhaa* to the Prayer-ground, and the first thing he would begin with was the Prayer. Then after finishing he would stand in front of the people and the people would be sitting in their rows. So he would admonish them, advise them and order them. If he wanted to send out an army for an expedition he would do so, or if he wanted to give some command he would do so, and then depart." Aboo Sa'eed said: "So this is how the people continued..."[132]

However it is unfortunate that the *'Eid* only increases us in our frivolity and negligence.

Also when rain ceases, cattle die and journeys cannot be accomplished them the Muslim turns to his Lord in Prayer and supplication, so mercy descends and rain pours down for the people.

---

[131] Reported by Ahmad, Muslim (Eng. trans. 2/450/2071) and others.

[132] Reported by al-Bukhaaree (Eng. trans. 2/40/no.76), Muslim (Eng. trans. 2/418/no.1931), and others and refer to the book *Salaatul-'Eidain fil-Musallaa* (The *'Eid* Prayer is to be Prayed on the Prayer-ground) by our Shaikh al-Albaanee *hafidhahullaah,* in which he says (p.18): "It contains a strong indication that the *'Eid Khutbah* is not restricted to the admonition and words of guidance, but that it also covers reminding and correction with regard to everything required for the well-being of the *Ummah.*"

From 'Abbaad ibn Tameem, from his uncle *radiyallaahu 'anhu*, "That the Prophet (ﷺ) invoked Allaah for rain and prayed two *rak'ahs*, and turned his cloak inside out."[133]

When the servant commits a sin he makes *wudoo* and perfects it and prays two *rak'ahs* and then asks Allaah to forgive his sin, with a sincere heart, and so Allaah, the Most High, forgives him.

From Aboo Bakr *radiyallaahu 'anhu*, who said that Allaah's Messenger (ﷺ) said: *There is no servant who commits a sin and therefore performs wudoo and perfects the purification, then stands and prays two rak'ahs, then asks Allaah to forgive that sin, except that Allaah forgives him.*[134]

It is also possible for the Muslim to pray the 'Prayer for a need' and to supplicate to Allaah, the One free of all imperfections and the Most High, whilst being certain that his supplication will be answered.

From 'Uthmaan ibn Haneef that a man with poor eyesight came to the Prophet (ﷺ) and said: *"Supplicate to Allaah for Him to cure me". So he said: If you wish I will delay it for you and that is better, and if you wish I will supplicate. So he said: 'Make supplication.' So he ordered him to make wudoo and to perfect the wudoo, and pray two rak'ahs and supplicate...*[135, 136]

---

[133] Reported by al-Bukhaaree (Eng. trans. 2/76/no.138).

[134] Reported by Ahmad, Aboo Daawood (Eng. trans. 1/396/no.1516) and the remaining three *Sunan* and it is found in *Saheehul-Jaami'* (no.5614).

[135] So a Muslim should supplicate according to his need and should not stick to a particular wording.

[136] From *Saheeh Ibn Maajah* (no.1137), and refer to the book *at-Tawassul wal-Waseelah* by Shaikhul-Islaam Ibn Taymiyyah *rahimahullaah*, and the book *at-Tawassul: its types*

As for the *Duhaa* (Forenoon) Prayer[137] then it is a means of increasing *eemaan*, and receiving a great reward from Allaah, the One free and far removed from all imperfections and the Most High. From this is:

(1) What is established from Aboo Hurairah *radiyallaahu 'anhu*, that he said: *Allaah's Messenger (ﷺ) sent an army and they captured a great amount of war booty and returned quickly. So a man said: O Messenger of Allaah we have never seen an army return more quickly nor having taken a greater amount of war booty than this army. So he said: Shall I not inform you of one who is quicker in returning and takes a larger booty? A man who makes wudoo and perfects wudoo, then goes off to the mosque and prays the Morning Prayer in it, then follows it up with the Duhaa (Forenoon) Prayer, he is quicker in returning and takes a larger booty.*[138]

(2) Also what Abud-Dardaa *radiyallaahu 'anhu*, reports from the Messenger of Allaah (ﷺ) that he said: *Whoever prays the Duhaa (Forenoon) Prayer as two rak'ahs then he will not be written amongst the negligent. Whoever prays four will be written amongst the worshippers. Whoever prays six will be given sufficiency through it for that day. Whoever prays eight then Allaah will write him amongst the obedient servants, and whoever prays twelve rak'ahs, then Allaah will build a house for him in Paradise, and there is no day or night except that Allaah showers extra favours upon His servants, and Allaah has not favoured any one of His*

= *and its rulings*, by our Shaikh al-Albaanee *hafidhahullaah*, (Al-Hidaayah Publishing and Distribution, 1995) since they explain clearly which types of *waseelah* are permissible and which are not.

[137] Translator's note: An optional Prayer after the sun has risen somewhat, until before the time of *Dhuhr*.

[138] Reported by Aboo Ya'laa and the narrators in his chain are those of the *Saheeh*, and by al-Bazzaar and Ibn Hibbaan in his *Saheeh*. It is found in *Saheehut-Targheeb* (no.667).

servants with anything better than that He guides him to His remembrance.[139]

(3) Likewise what Aboo Hurairah *radiyallaahu 'anhu*, reports from the Messenger of Allaah (ﷺ) that he said: *None are constant in praying the Duhaa Prayer except the penitent. He said: And it is the Prayer of the penitent (al-Awwaabeen).*[140, 141]

Likewise if a servant commits a sin, but then stands up, performs the purification and prays, then asks for Allaah's forgiveness, then Allaah, the Most High, forgives him. Just as Aboo Bakr *radiyallaahu 'anhu*, reports that I heard Allaah's Messenger (ﷺ) say: *There is not a man who commits a sin, then stands and performs the purification, then prays, then seeks Allaah's forgiveness except that Allaah forgives him*. Then he recited this *Aayah*:

وَٱلَّذِينَ إِذَا فَعَلُوا۟ فَٰحِشَةً أَوْ ظَلَمُوٓا۟ أَنفُسَهُمْ ذَكَرُوا۟ ٱللَّهَ

"And those who, when they have committed illegal sexual intercourse or wronged themselves with evil, remember Allaah..."[142]

to the end of the Aayah.[143]

---

[139] Reported by at-Tabaraanee in *al-Kabeer* and its narrators are reliable and it occurs in *Saheehut-Targheeb* (no.674).

[140] *Al-Awwaabeen* are those who frequently turn in repentance to Allaah, the Most High.

[141] Reported by at-Tabaraanee and Ibn Khuzaimah in his *Saheeh* and is found in *Saheehut-Targheeb* (no.676).

[142] Soorah Aal-'Imraan (3):135

[143] Reported by at-Tirmidhee who declared it to be *hasan*, and it is reported by Aboo Daawood (Eng. trans. 1/396/no.1516), an-Nasaa'ee and Ibn Maajah and it is found in *Saheehut-Targheeb* (no.680).

With regard to *Salaatut-Tasbeeh* there is a huge reward mentioned about it, and forgiveness of sins and increase of *eemaan*. Indeed through it Allaah, the Most High, will forgive your sins, the first and the last of them, old and new sins, mistakes and what was deliberate, lesser and greater sins, what was hidden and what was done openly. This is as is established from Ibn 'Abbaas *radiyallaahu 'anhu*, that the Prophet (ﷺ) said: *O 'Abbaas! O my uncle! Shall I not give you, shall I not bestow upon you, shall I not donate to you? Shall I not produce in you ten things, if you do that then Allaah will forgive your sins, their first and their last, old and new, mistakes and deliberate errors, small and great, hidden and open? Ten things. You should pray four rak'ahs, reciting in each rak'ah the Opening of the Book (Faatihatul-Kitaab) and a Soorah. Then when you have finished reciting in the first rak'ah and you are standing you should say fifteen times subhaanallaah (Allaah is free from all imperfections), al-hamdu lillaah (all praise is for Allaah), La ilaaha illallaah (none has the right to be worshipped except Allaah) and Allaahu Akbar (Allaah is greater). Then you should bow and say it in rukoo' and say it ten times, then raise up your head from the rukoo' and say it ten times, then prostrate and say it whilst you are in prostration (sujood) ten times, then raise up your head from the prostration and say it ten times, then prostrate and say it ten times, then raise up your head and say it ten times. So that will be seventy-five times in every rak'ah, which you do in four rak'ahs. So if your sins were like the foam of the sea, or like heaped sand, then Allaah would forgive them for you. If you are able to pray it once every day, then do so. If not then once in every week. If not then once in every month. If not then once in every year. If not then once in your lifetime.*[144]

---

[144] Reported by Aboo Daawood (Eng. trans. 1/340/no.1292), an-Nasaa'ee, Ibn Maajah and others and it is found in *Saheehul-Jaami'* (no.7814).

11. The Prayer of the Weak and its Connection with Aid and Victory for the *Ummah*

From Sa'd *radiyallaahu 'anhu*, who said that Allaah's Messenger (ﷺ) said: *Indeed Allaah aids this Ummah due to its weak ones, through their supplication, their Prayer and their purity of intention.*[145]

So with this the inferiority of the people's thinking is clear, those who say: Give your attention to the rich, the powerful and the people of standing and leave the poor. We have indeed abandoned the weak, the poor, those in poverty, and the pious, and we have tasted the bitterness of defeat, of humiliation and of ruin. Why shouldn't this be our predicament when victory of this *Ummah* was tied to their supplication, their Prayer and their purity of intention? So let us take care to keep the company of the weak and the pious, and seek victory from Allaah, the One free and far removed from all imperfections and the Most High, asking them to supplicate for the removal of our suffering and the suffering of the *Ummah* of Muhammad (ﷺ).

---

[145] Reported by an-Nasaa'ee and others, and it is found in al-Bukhaaree and other places without mention of purity of intention. It is found in *Saheehut-Targheeb* (no.5).

12. In Prayer Lies Tranquillity and Peace of Mind

Through the Prayer tranquillity, peace of mind and joyfulness come about since the person feels that he is near to Allaah, the Most High. He, the One free and far removed from all imperfections, says:

"Say: 'Verily, Allaah sends astray whom He wills and guides unto Himself those who turn to Him in repentance.' Those who believe, and whose hearts find rest in the remembrance of Allaah. Verily, in the remembrance of Allaah do hearts find rest." [146]

The whole of the Prayer is remembrance of Allaah and supplication. The Prophet (ﷺ) also used to say to Bilaal: *O Bilaal! Give the call for establishment of the Prayer. Give us comfort by it.*[147]

He (ﷺ) said: *And the Prayer was made the coolness of my eyes.*[148, 149]

So awaken, O seeker after happiness, contentment and that which is a `coolness for the eyes, and give your attention to the Prayer with atten-

---

[146] Soorah ar-Ra'd (13):27-28

[147] Reported by Ahmad and Aboo Daawood (Eng. trans. 3/1388/no.4967) and is found in *Saheehul-Jaami'* (no.7769).

[148] Translator's note: i.e. that which was most pleasing to him.

[149] Reported by Ahmad, an-Nasaa'ee and others and it is found in *Saheehul-Jaami'* (no.3093).

tiveness and humility before Allaah, the Most High, just as it was prayed by Allaah's Messenger (ﷺ) before us. Only then will you achieve what you long for, otherwise blame no one but yourself.

13. Lessons from the Prophet's (ﷺ) Last Illness

From 'Ubaydullaah ibn 'Abdullaah who said: *I entered upon 'Aa'ishah and said to her: Will you not inform me of the illness of the Messenger of Allaah (ﷺ)? She said: Indeed yes. It became severe upon the Prophet (ﷺ), so he said: Have the people prayed? We said: No, and they are waiting for you O Messenger of Allaah! He said: Put water in the tub for me. So we did so, and he bathed and tried to stand up, but fainted. Then he regained consciousness and said: Have the people prayed? We said: No, and they are waiting for you O Messenger of Allaah! So he said: Put water in the tub for me. So we did so, and he bathed and tried to stand up, but fainted. Then he regained consciousness and said: Have the people prayed? We said: No, and they are waiting for you O Messenger of Allaah! So he said: Put water in the tub for me. So we did so, and he bathed and tried to stand up, but fainted. Then he regained consciousness and said: Have the people prayed? We said: No, and they are waiting for you O Messenger of Allaah! She ('Aa'ishah) said: And the people were gathered in the mosque, waiting for Allaah's Messenger (ﷺ) for the last 'Ishaa Prayer. She said: So Allaah's Messenger (ﷺ) sent the message to Aboo Bakr that he should lead the people in Prayer. So the messenger came to him and said: Allaah's Messenger (ﷺ) orders you to lead the people in the Prayer. So Aboo Bakr said, and he was a soft hearted man: O 'Umar lead the people in the Prayer. So 'Umar replied: You have more right to that. She ('Aa'ishah) said: So Aboo Bakr lead them in the Prayer in those days. Then Allaah's Messenger (ﷺ) found some improvement in his condition and so he went out supported by two men, one of whom was al-'Abbaas, for the Dhuhr Prayer, and Aboo Bakr was leading the people in Prayer. So when Aboo Bakr saw him he started to move back, but the Prophet (ﷺ) indicated to him that he should not move back, and he said to the two men: Sit me at his side. So they sat him down beside Aboo Bakr and Aboo Bakr prayed standing following the Prayer of the Prophet (ﷺ), and the people prayed following the Prayer of Aboo Bakr, and the Prophet (ﷺ) was sitting.*[150]

From 'Alee *radiyallaahu 'anhu*, who said: The last words of the Prophet (ﷺ) were: *The Prayer, the Prayer, and fear Allaah with regard to what your right hands possess.*[151]

Consider the attention and importance which the Prophet (ﷺ) gave to the Prayer of the Muslims in the illness from which he died. Every time he came round from being unconscious he asked: *Have the people prayed*? This occured four times. Then when he found some improvement in his condition he was anxious to pray with the congregation and to meet his Companions *radiyallaahu 'anhum*, so he went out supported by two of his Companions *radiyallaahu 'anhum*. So what occurred at the time of the final illness of the Prophet (ﷺ) shows the importance of the Prayer, and of the congregation, and the position which the mosque holds in Islaam.

So he gave attention and importance to the Prayer even during the illness from which he died! So what about you, O healthy and fit? What about you, O youths? What about you who have been blessed with strength and vigour? How can you be pleased with staying away from the mosque and the congregation? How then will you treat the Prayer when you become ill?

O Muslim "The Prayer, The Prayer," the last thing which the Prophet (ﷺ) said, and the first thing which the servant will be accountable for on the Day of Resurrection. So fear Allaah with regard to your own souls, and take account of yourselves before you are taken to account.

---

[150] Reported by Muslim (Eng. trans. 1/228/no.832)

[151] Reported by Aboo Daawood (Eng. trans. 3/1425/no.5137) and Ibn Maajah, and it is found in *Saheehul-Jaami'* (no.4492).

14. Allaah Sent Down Wealth in Order that the Prayer be Established and the Zakaat be Paid

This heading may appear strange, but this strangeness will be removed when we know that it has been extracted from a saying of the Prophet (ﷺ): *Indeed Allaah, the Most High, said: 'We have sent down the wealth for the Prayer to be established, and Zakaat to be given, and if the son of Aadam had a valley he would love to have a second, and if he had two valleys he would love to have a third, and nothing will fill the belly of the son of Aadam except dust, then Allaah will forgive whoever repents to Him.*[152]

It will help our understanding of this noble *hadeeth* to know that the purpose behind the creation of man and *jinn* is the worship of Allaah, the One free and far removed from all imperfections and the Most High, nothing else as He, the Most perfect, says:

وَمَا خَلَقْتُ ٱلْجِنَّ وَٱلْإِنسَ إِلَّا لِيَعْبُدُونِ ﴿٥٦﴾

> **"I have not created the *jinn* and men except that they should worship Me."**[153]

So everything else is merely a means to be used by *jinn* and men to achieve obedience to Allaah, everything, such as food, drink, riding-beast, marriage and wealth. So wealth was not sent down except for the fulfilment of the worship of Allaah, so that his body can be strengthened through food and drink and thus enable him to establish the Prayer. He may also

[152] Reported by Ahmad and at-Tabaraanee in *al-Kabeer* from Aboo Waaqid *radiyallaahu 'anhu*, and it occurs in *Saheebul-Jaami'* (no.1777).

[153] Soorah adh-Dhaariyaat (51):56

use it to marry, and marriage is also "half of the religion"[154] or, "half of *eemaan*."[155] Marriage helps the servant to restrain his glance, and to protect his private parts. So if the married servant stands to pray to Allaah, the Most High, then his humility and attentiveness is stronger, and his heart more heedful of Allaah, the Most High, since failure to restrain ones glance and protect ones private parts kills off his humility and attentiveness.

The Muslim may also use his wealth to cure himself so that his body is strengthened and so his performance of the Prayer will be better than that of the sick.

Thus wealth which has been sent down is either for the establishment of the Prayer, or to assist in that, or for the payment of the *Zakaat* and to help those in need.

However the son of Aadam is ignorant, or pretends to be ignorant, to the point that if he had a whole valley of wealth then he would love to have a second. Then if he attained what he hoped for and acquired a second, he would love to have a third.

The son of Aadam has forgotten the reason for which wealth was sent down, which was the establishment of Prayer and payment of the *Zakaat*, and instead involved himself with large business concerns and has become drowned in the sea of materialism. All of this due to the first valley so how will he manage to attain the second and the third?

---

[154] As he (ﷺ) said: "*When the servant marries then he has completed half of the religion. Then let him fear Allaah with regard to the remaining half.*" Reported by al-Baihaqee in *Shu'abul-Eemaan*, and it is found in *Saheehul-Jaami'* (no.443).

[155] As he (ﷺ) said: "*Whoever marries has completed half of eemaan, so let him fear Allaah with regard to the remaining half.*" *Saheehul-Jaami'* (no.6024).

How much concentration and humility (*khushoo'*) he misses in the Prayer due to this excessive toil, seeking to attain something extra in this world whilst losing a huge amount of good.

Then the matter does not stop at him losing *khushoo'* alone, rather it extends into him missing the Prayers. So you see those who miss the Prayers due to their preoccupation with amassing wealth, forgetting that wealth is only for the Prayer and for the *Zakaat*, and Allaah's Messenger (ﷺ) said: *If I had the like of (mount) Uhud in gold it would not please me that three days would pass me by and anything of it remained with me, except for something which I kept for payment of debts.*[156]

Furthermore from the widespread afflictions is that you hear people giving religious verdicts that are pleasing to those preoccupied with wealth, and that is that it is permissible to combine all the five Prayers together, so they delay all the Prayers and pray them after *'Ishaa* and throw aside the Prayer times and related obligations. Indeed there is no ability and no action except by the will of Allaah.

---

[156] Reported by al-Bukhaaree (Eng. trans. 8/303/452) from Aboo Hurairah *radiyallaahu 'anhu*.

15. Those Who Abandon the Prayer

Through the Prayer *eemaan* is increased and likewise leaving it causes its decrease, and if the person abandons it totally then he has fallen into *kufr* and *shirk*.[157]

From Jaabir *radiyallaahu 'anhu*, who said that Allaah's Messenger (ﷺ) said: *Between kufr and eemaan lies abandonment of the Prayer.*[158] From him also, that he said that Allaah's Messenger (ﷺ) said: *Between a man and between shirk and kufr there is abandonment of the Prayer.*[159]

There occurs in *Saheehul-Bukhaaree* from Anas ibn Maalik *radiyallaahu 'anhu*: *"That when the Prophet (ﷺ) went out with us to fight any people he would not attack until morning and he would wait. So if he heard the adhaan he would leave them, but if he did not hear the adhaan he would attack them."*[160]

---

[157] This matter requires elaboration, since if the person rejects the Prayer with his heart then he has left the religion of Islaam. Otherwise it is a case of *kufr* less than *kufr*, or if you wish then *kufr* of action, in that he has resembled the *kuffaar* in action.

[158] Reported by at-Tirmidhee and it occurs in *Saheehul-Jaami'* (no.2846).

[159] Reported by Muslim (Eng. trans. 1/48/no.146), Aboo Daawood (Eng. trans. 3/1311/no.4661), at-Tirmidhee and Ibn Maajah.

[160] Reported by al-Bukhaaree (Eng. trans. 1/337/no.584) and it is reported with wording close to this by Muslim (Eng. trans. 1/209/no.745).

16. One Who Misses the Prayer

From Nawfal ibn Mu'aawiyah *radiyallaahu 'anhu*, that the Prophet (ﷺ) said: *Whoever missed the Prayer, then it as if he had lost his family and his wealth.*[161]

How would you feel, O Muslim brother, if you were to lose your precious son? How would you feel if you lost your wife? What pain would you feel if you lost your family? What would your grief be like if you lost both your family and your wealth? Indeed it would be an agonising blow and terrible grief that a person should lose his family and wealth. Losing his family with whom he lived with and experienced much joy. The spacious earth would seem constricted for one who lost his family. He would experience distress, grief and agony. Then how about one who in addition lost his wealth? Fresh and sweet wealth which Allaah made a support for us, how would you feel if that occurred also? Then know that one who misses the Prayer has indeed suffered a huge loss.

---

[161] Reported by Ibn Hibbaan in his *Saheeh* and it occurs in *Saheehut-Targheeb* (no.576).

17. Training Oneself Upon Having *Khushoo'* in the Prayer

It may be that you pray behind an *imaam* who fulfils the very minimum with regard to *khushoo'* in the pillars of the Prayer. So what is the way to increase one's own *khushoo'*? One will have to seize the opportunity at other times and Prayers other than the obligatory Prayer. So take the opportunity provided by the *sunnah* and optional (*nawaafil*) Prayers, since they are a very great means of training oneself upon *khushoo'*. Accustom yourself to lengthening the recitation[162] and the standing, and concerning this he (ﷺ) said: *The best Prayer is that in which there is lengthy standing.*[163]

Also make the bowing and the prostration long, and supplicate much whilst in prostration, and remember that Allaah's Messenger (ﷺ) sought refuge from the lack of *khushoo'*, saying: *O Allaah I seek Your refuge from a heart which does not have khushoo'.*[164]

---

[162] Except where it is prescribed not to do so, such as the recitation in the *rak'ahs* of the *sunnah* Prayer before *Fajr*, and refer to *The Prophet's* (ﷺ) *Prayer Described* (p.31).

[163] Reported by Muslim (Eng. trans. 1/364/1652) and others.

[164] Reported by at-Tirmidhee, an-Nasaa'ee and others, and it occurs in *Saheehul-Jaami'* (no.1308).

18. Things Which are Detrimental to *Khushoo'*[165]

(1) Weakness of *eemaan* in the meeting with Allaah, the Most High, and that one will indeed return to Him.

Allaah, the Most High, says:

وَٱسْتَعِينُوا۟ بِٱلصَّبْرِ وَٱلصَّلَوٰةِ ۚ وَإِنَّهَا لَكَبِيرَةٌ إِلَّا عَلَى ٱلْخَٰشِعِينَ ﴿٤٥﴾ ٱلَّذِينَ يَظُنُّونَ أَنَّهُم مُّلَٰقُوا۟ رَبِّهِمْ وَأَنَّهُمْ إِلَيْهِ رَٰجِعُونَ ﴿٤٦﴾

"And seek help in patience and prayer and truly it is heavy except for those humble themselves (before Allaah). (They are those) who are certain that they are going to meet their Lord, and that unto Him they are going to return."[166]

Allaah, the Most High, has described the attributes of the possessors of *khushoo'* and that they are those who are certain that they are going to meet their Lord, the One free and far removed from all imperfections, and that they will return to Him.

This is certain knowledge of the meeting with Allaah and of the return to Him. So any deficiency in this will be a deficiency in ones *khushoo'*. Whereas correct belief in this regard will cause you to judge the matter correctly so that you perfect your Prayer and correct your conduct.

---

[165] I have mentioned some things in this section without further details or evidences since they have already preceded in the book.

[166] Soorah al-Baqarah (2):45-46

(2) Whisperings of Satan.

From Aboo Hurairah *radiyallaabu 'anbu*, that Allaah's Messenger (ﷺ) said: *When the call to Prayer is given, Satan goes off passing wind so that he does not hear the adhaan, then when the call is finished he returns. Then when the iqaamah is given he goes off, until when the iqaamah is finished he returns in order to interfere with the person and his concentration, he says: 'Remember such and such', referring to things which the man was not thinking of, to the point the man does not know how much he has prayed.*[167]

(3) Neglectfulness and desires.

(4) Giving undue attention to this world.

(5) Avoiding the mosque and the congregation, as he (ﷺ) said: *Indeed the wolf eats the lone sheep.*[168]

(6) Weakness of the love for one's brother for the sake of Allaah, as he (ﷺ) said: *By Him in whose Hand is my soul you will not enter Paradise until you have eemaan, and you will not have eemaan until you love each other. Shall I not guide you to an action which if you do it you will come to love one another? Spread the (greeting of) salaam between yourselves.*[169]

(7) Failing to straighten the rows and close any gaps.

---

[167] Reported by al-Bukhaaree (Eng. trans. 2/181/no.323) and Muslim (Eng. trans. 1/211/no.756).

[168] The *hadeeth* has preceded.

[169] Reported by Muslim and others from Aboo Hurairah, and it has preceded.

(8) Oppressing others and failing to give them their due rights.

(9) Turning aside, and looking towards the sky.

From Qataadah, that Anas ibn Maalik narrated to them, saying that the Prophet (ﷺ) said: *What is the matter with a people who raise their gaze to the sky whilst in Prayer?* and his saying about that was severe to the point that he said: *They will indeed stop this, otherwise their sight will be snatched away.*[170]

From Aboo Hurairah *radiyallaahu 'anhu*, who said that Allaah's Messenger (ﷺ) said: *A people will indeed stop raising their gaze to the sky whilst supplicating in the Prayer, otherwise their sight will be snatched away.*[171]

From Ibn 'Umar *radiyallaahu 'anhu*, who said that Allaah's Messenger (ﷺ) said: *Do not raise your gaze to the sky whilst in Prayer since it may be snatched away.*[172]

Also in the *hadeeth*: *...Allaah commands you with the Prayer so when you pray then do not turn aside, since Allaah turns His Face to the face of His servant in his Prayer, as long as he does not turn aside.*[173]

---

[170] Reported by al-Bukhaaree (Eng. trans. 1/401/717).

[171] Reported by Muslim (Eng. trans. 1/236/no.863).

[172] Reported by Ibn Maajah and at-Tabaraanee and it occurs in *Saheehul-Jaami'* (no.7157).

[173] Part of a *hadeeth* reported by at-Tirmidhee who declared it to be *hasan saheeh* and it occurs in *Saheehut-Targheeb* (no.553).

(10) Prayer upon something ornamented, decorated or containing pictures.

From 'Aa'ishah *radiyallaahu 'anhaa*: *The Prophet* (ﷺ) *prayed in a square cloak having markings and he glanced at it so when he finished he said: Take this cloak of mine to Aboo Jahm and bring me the plain coarse cloak of Aboo Jahm, since it has just distracted me from my Prayer.*[174]

Also from 'Aa'ishah *radiyallaahu 'anhaa*, who said that the Prophet (ﷺ) said: *I was looking at its markings during the Prayer and I fear that it will divert me.*[175]

From Anas *radiyallaahu 'anhu*, who said: 'Aa'ishah had a thin colourful curtain with which she screened one side of her home, so the Prophet (ﷺ) said: *Remove this curtain of yours from us since its pictures do not cease to appear before me in the Prayer.*[176]

---

[174] Reported by al-Bukhaaree (Eng. trans. 1/226/no.369).

[175] Reported by al-Bukhaaree (Eng. trans. 1/226/no.370).

[176] Reported by al-Bukhaaree (Eng. trans. 1/226/no.371).

19. Some Important Points

(1) Give importance, may Allaah preserve you, to the performance of the *nafl* and *sunnah* Prayers before and after the obligatory Prayer, since they make up for any deficiency in the obligatory Prayer, as he (ﷺ) said: *The first thing for which the servant will have to account on the Day of Resurrection is his Prayer. So if he has completed it, then it is written as complete for him. But if he has not completed it, then Allaah will say to His angels: 'See, do you find any optional Prayers for My servant so that you may complete his obligatory Prayer with them?' Then the Zakaat, then the rest of the actions will be dealt with accordingly.*[177]

From 'Aa'idh ibn Qurt *radiyallaahu 'anhu*, who said that Allaah's Messenger (ﷺ) said: *Whoever prays a Prayer which he does not perfect, then it will be added to from his optional Prayers until it is perfected.*[178]

(2) Give importance to catching the initial *Takbeer*, particularly for forty days running, since this will free the servant from hypocrisy and from the Fire, if Allaah wills. This is shown by what is narrated by Anas *radiyallaahu 'anhu*, from Allaah's Messenger (ﷺ) that he said: *Whoever prays for Allaah for forty days in congregation, reaching the first takbeer, then two declarations of freedom are written for him: freedom from the Fire and freedom from hypocrisy.*[179]

---

[177] Reported by Ahmad, Aboo Daawood (Eng. trans. 1/221-222/nos.863 & 865), Ibn Maajah and al-Haakim from Tameem ad-Daaree and it is *hasan*, see *Saheehul-Jaami'* (no.2571).

[178] Reported by at-Tabaraanee in *al-Kabeer* and it is found in *Saheehul-Jaami'* (no.6224).

[179] Reported by at-Tirmidhee and it is found in *Saheehul-Jaami'* (no.6241).

(3) Give your houses a share of your Prayers, since that will produce a great deal of good for you, as is established from Jaabir *radiyallaahu 'anhu*, that he said that Allaah's Messenger (ﷺ) said: *When one of you has completed the Prayer in the mosque, then let him give a share of his Prayer to his house, since through his Prayer Allaah will place good on his house.*[180]

Also in another *hadeeth*: *Pray, O people, in your houses since the most excellent Prayer is a person's Prayer in his house, except for the obligatory Prayer.*[181]

In another *hadeeth*: *The Prayer of one of you in his house is better than his Prayer in my mosque except for the obligatory Prayer.*[182]

So this is the case with regard to optional Prayer in one's house, it is better than Prayer in the mosque of the Prophet (ﷺ), along with the increased reward therein, and Prayer in his mosque is equal to a thousand Prayers.[183]

The excellence of the optional Prayer in the house is like the excellence of the obligatory Prayer over the optional Prayer. This is shown by way of Suhayb ibn an-Nu'maan *radiyallaahu 'anhu*, who narrates from the Prophet (ﷺ) that he said: *The excellence of a man's Prayer in his house*

---

[180] Reported by Muslim (Eng. trans. 1/376/no.1705) and others.

[181] Reported by al-Bukhaaree (Eng. trans. 1/391/no.698) and others.

[182] Reported by Aboo Daawood (Eng. trans. 1/268/no.1039) and others and it is found in *Saheehul-Jaami'* (no.3708).

[183] As he (ﷺ) said: *A Prayer in this mosque of mine is better than a thousand Prayers in other mosques, except for Masjidul-Haraam*. Reported by Muslim (Eng. trans. 2/697/no.3209) and others.

over his Prayer where the people can see him is like the excellence of the obligatory over the optional Prayer.[184]

(4) Do not neglect perfection of the *rukoo'* (bowing) and the *sujood* (prostration), in order that you do not become the greatest thief as occurs in his (ﷺ) saying: *The greatest thief amongst the people is the one who steals from his Prayer, not completing its rukoo' and sujood, and the most miserly of people is the one who is miserly about giving the (greeting of) salaam.*[185]

I cannot find a more expressive word than 'the greatest thief' to show the vileness of one who does not complete the *rukoo'* and the *sujood*, since stealing is something blameworthy by agreement, both in the *sharee'ah* and in man's nature, and the thief when committing the sin is taking from someone else. So by making the *rukoo'* and the *sujood* defective the person has taken that which is not his, since the Prayer is Allaah's, not the person's. Since this is done before its owner and it is easy for the person to take what he pleases without any fear or worry that the people will find out, then it is deserving that he is called the greatest thief.

However do not forget that he who does not complete the *rukoo'* and the *sujood* is under the threat that he will die upon other than the religion, and we seek Allaah the Most High's refuge from that, due to what is narrated by Waasil ibn Abee Waa'il, from Hudhayfah *radiyallaahu 'anhu*, that he saw a man that was not completing the *rukoo'* and the *sujood*, so when he finished his Prayer, Hudhayfah said to him: "You have not prayed," and I think that he said: "If you were to die then you would die

---

[184] Reported by at-Tabaraanee in *al-Kabeer* and al-Baihaqee in his *Sunan* and others and is found in *Saheehul-Jaami'* (no.4093).

[185] Reported by at-Tabaraanee in *al-Awsat* from 'Abdullaah ibn Mughaffal *radiyallaahu 'anhu*, and it occurs in *Saheehul-Jaami'* (no.977).

upon other than the *Sunnah* of Muhammad (ﷺ)."[186]

(5) Give importance to praying in the first row in the mosque since it is the best of the rows as occurs in the *hadeeth*: *The best of the rows of the men is the first, and the worst is the last, and the best of the rows of the women is the last and the worst is the first.*[187]

Also a person does not continue to keep himself back from the first row except that Allaah, the Most High, keeps him back in the Fire, even if he is a person of Paradise. As he (ﷺ) said: *A people will not cease keeping themselves back from the first row except that Allaah will keep them back in the Fire.*[188]

From Aboo Sa'eed al-Khudree *radiyallaahu 'anhu*, that Allaah's Messenger (ﷺ) saw that some of his Companions remained at the back, so he said to them: *Move forward, and follow me, and let them who come after you follow you. A people will not cease to remain at the back except that Allaah will place them at the back.*[189]

---

[186] Reported by al-Bukhaaree (Eng. trans. 1/430/no.772) and then one of the noble brothers reminded me of a *hadeeth* from the Prophet (ﷺ) about that, so I referred back to it and its wording is: *"That Allaah's Messenger (ﷺ) saw a man praying and he did not complete the rukoo' and quickly pecked the sujood, so he said: If this one were to die upon this state he would die upon other than the religion of Muhammad."* It is reported by Aboo Ya'laa in his *Musnad* and Ibn 'Asaakir with *hasan* chain of narration, and it is declared *saheeh* by Ibn Khuzaimah and others and is found in *The Prophet's Prayer Described* (p.44).

[187] Reported by Muslim (Eng. trans. 1/239/881), Aboo Daawood (Eng. trans. 1/175/no.678) and at-Tirmidhee and others.

[188] Reported by Aboo Daawood (Eng. trans. 1/175/no.679) and declared *saheeh* by Ibn Khuzaimah and Ibn Hibbaan and it is found in *Saheehul-Jaami'* (no.7576).

[189] Reported by Muslim (Eng. trans. 1/239/878) and others.

Also in the *hadeeth*: *Be present for the Jumu'ah and be close to the imaam, since a person will not cease keeping himself back until Allaah keeps him back in Paradise even if he enters it.*[190]

From Aboo Hurairah *radiyallaahu 'anhu*, that Allaah's Messenger (ﷺ) said: *If the people knew what (reward) there is in the call and first row and then found no way to get it except to draw lots for it they would do so, and if they knew what (reward) there was in coming early to the Prayer they would race with each other for it, and if they knew what (reward) there was in the 'Atamah (i.e. 'Ishaa) Prayer and the Subh (i.e. Fajr) Prayer they would come to them even if they had to crawl.*[191]

From Aboo Hurairah *radiyallaahu 'anhu*, also, who said that Allaah's Messenger (ﷺ) said: *If you knew (or they knew) what (reward) there was in the front row then they would draw lots for it.*[192]

(6) Give importance to praying behind an *imaam* who gives the recitation its due, both its amount and in how he recites, so that fulfils the rules of correct recitation, and has a good voice which produces an effect upon the people. But if this is not to be found at the mosque near to you, then seek it in a different mosque even if it is only for some of the Prayers. This is because a beautiful voice increases the Qur'aan in beauty as occurs in the *hadeeth* narrated by al-Baraa' *radiyallaahu 'anhu*, from the Prophet

---

[190] Reported by Ahmad, Aboo Daawood (Eng. trans. 1/285/no.1103) and others and is found in *Saheehul-Jaami'* (no.198).

[191] Reported by al-Bukhaaree (Eng. trans. 1/353/no.624) and Muslim (Eng. trans. 1/239/877) and others.

[192] Reported by Muslim (Eng. trans. 1/239/no.880) and Ibn Maajah.

(ﷺ) that he said: *Adorn the Qur'aan with your voices, since a beautiful voice increases the Qur'aan in beauty.*[193]

From Jaabir *radiyallaahu 'anhu*, who said that Allaah's Messenger (ﷺ) said: *From the people having the best voice in reciting the Qur'aan is the one who when you hear him recite then you consider that he fears Allaah.*[194]

---

[193] Reported by Aboo Daawood (Eng. trans. 1/384/no.1463) and others and is found in *Saheehul-Jaami'* (no.3575).

[194] Reported by Ibn Maajah and it occurs in *Saheehul-Jaami'* (no.2198).

20. The Excellence of Prayer in Particular Mosques

(1) Excellence of the Prayer in *al-Masjidul-Haraam* and *al-Masjidun-Nabawee.*[195]

From Ibn az-Zubayr *radiyallaabu 'anbu*, who said that Allaah's Messenger (ﷺ) said: *A Prayer in this mosque of mine is better than a thousand Prayers in other mosques, except for al-Masjidul-Haraam, and a Prayer in al-Masjidul-Haraam is better by a hundred times than a Prayer in this mosque of mine.*[196]

(2) Excellence of Prayer in *al-Masjid al-Aqsaa*[197]

He (ﷺ) said: *Journey is not to be undertaken except to three mosques: al-Masjidul-Haraam, this mosque of mine, and al-Masjidul-Aqsaa.*[198]

From 'Abdullaah ibn 'Amr from the Prophet (ﷺ) who said: *When Sulaymaan ibn Daawood finished the rebuilding of Baitul-Maqdis*[199] *he asked Allaah for three things: For judgement which agreed with His judgement, and for dominion none should deserve after him, and that no one should come to this mosque, intending only Prayer in it, except that he would be cleansed of sins just as he was on the day when his mother*

---

[195] Translator's note: The mosque in Makkah and the Prophet's mosque in al-Madeenah respectively.

[196] Reported by Ahmad and declared *saheeh* by Ibn Hibbaan, and it occurs in *Saheebul-Jaami'* (no.3735).

[197] Translator's note: In Jerusalem.

[198] Reported by al-Bukhaaree (Eng. trans. 2/157/no.181) and Muslim (Eng. trans. 2/699/no.3218).

[199] Translator's note: The Jerusalem mosque.

gave birth to him. The Prophet (ﷺ) said: As for two of these, then they were granted to him and I hope that he will also be granted the third.[200]

(3) Excellence of the Qubaa[201]

From Sahl ibn Hunayf *radiyallaahu 'anhu*, who said that Allaah's Messenger (ﷺ) said: *Whoever purifies himself in his house, then comes to Qubaa mosque and prays in it, then he will have a reward like that of an 'Umrah.*[202]

[200] *Saheeh Ibn Maajah* (no.1156).

[201] Translator's note: A mosque in the south of al-Madeenah.

[202] Reported by Ahmad, Ibn Maajah and others and is found in *Saheehul-Jaami'* (no.6030).

21. The Excellence of Walking to the Mosque

From Aboo Hurairah *radiyallaahu 'anhu*, who said that Allaah's Messenger (ﷺ) said: *A man's Prayer with the congregation is twenty-five times better than his Prayer in his house and his market. That is because when he makes wudoo and perfects the wudoo, then goes out to the mosques, not going out except for the Prayer, then he does not take a step except that because of it he is raised by one rank, and one sin is removed from him. Then when he prays the angels do not cease supplicating for him, as long as he remains at his place of Prayer: 'O Allaah send blessings upon him, O Allaah have mercy upon him,' and he remains in Prayer as long as he waits for the Prayer.*[203] In a narration: '... *O Allaah forgive him.' For as long as he does not harm anyone or break his state of purification.*[204]

From 'Uqbah ibn 'Aamir *radiyallaahu 'anhu*, who said that the Prophet (ﷺ) said: *When a man purifies himself, then comes to the mosque to observe the Prayer, then his two scribes, or his scribe, write for him ten good deeds for every step which he takes to the mosque. Also the one sitting awaiting the Prayer is like one standing obediently in Prayer and is written amongst those who are praying, from when he leaves his house until he returns to it.*[205]

From 'Abdullaah ibn 'Amr *radiyallaahu 'anhumaa*, who said that Allaah's Messenger (ﷺ) said: *Whoever goes out to the congregational*

---

[203] Reported by al-Bukhaaree (Eng. trans. 1/352/no.620).

[204] Reported by Muslim (Eng. trans. 1/322/no.1394) and Aboo Daawood (Eng. trans. 1/147/no.559).

[205] Reported by Ahmad, Aboo Ya'laa, at-Tabaraanee in *al-Kabeer* and *al-Awsat* and others and it is found in *Saheehut-Targheeb* (no.297).

mosque then one footstep wipes away a sin, and the other footstep causes a good deed to be written, going and returning.[206]

From Jaabir *radiyallaahu 'anhu*, who said: *"Some plots of land were available around the mosque so Banoo Salamah wanted to move nearer to the mosque, so that reached the Prophet (ﷺ) so he said to them: It has reached me that you want to move near to the mosque. They said: 'Yes, O Messenger of Allaah! We wanted to do that.' So he said: O Banoo Salamah! Remain in your homes, your footsteps will be written. Remain in your homes your footsteps will be written. They said: 'We would not have been more pleased than this had we moved.'*[207] In a narration: *There is a rank for you for every footstep.*[208]

From Aboo Moosa *radiyallaahu 'anhu*, who said that Allaah's Messenger (ﷺ) said: *The people who receive the greatest reward for the Prayer are those who have to walk the furthest distance, then those who are next furthest. Also the one who waits to pray the Prayer along with the imaam has greater reward than one who prays it and then goes to sleep.*[209]

From Aboo Hurairah *radiyallaahu 'anhu*, who said that Allaah's Messenger (ﷺ) said: *Upon every joint of the people a charity is due on every day on which the sun rises. So bringing about justice between two people is a charity, and helping a man with his riding beast, that you*

---

[206] Reported by Ahmad with *hasan* chain of narration and at-Tabaraanee and declared *saheeh* by Ibn Hibbaan.

[207] Reported by Muslim (Eng. trans. 1/324/1408) and others.

[208] Reported by Muslim (Eng. trans. 1/324/no.1406).

[209] Reported by al-Bukhaaree (Eng. trans. 1/353/no.623) and Muslim (Eng. trans. 1/323/1401) and others.

help him onto it or that you raise up his provisions onto it for him, is a charity, and a good word is charity, and every footstep which you take walking to the mosque is a charity, and removing that which is harmful from the path is a charity.[210]

From Aboo Hurairah *radiyallaahu 'anhu*, who said that Allaah's Messenger (ﷺ) said: *Shall I not guide you to that by which Allaah will wipe away sins and through which He will raise peoples ranks? They said: 'Indeed yes, O Messenger of Allaah!' He said: Completing the wudoo when it is a hardship, taking many steps to the mosques, and waiting for the Prayer after the Prayer. That is persevering in obedience (ar-Ribaat),*[211] *that is persevering in obedience, that is persevering in obedience.*[212]

From Aboo Hurairah *radiyallaahu 'anhu*, who said that Allaah's Messenger (ﷺ) said: *Whoever goes out to the mosque in the morning or the evening then Allaah will prepare a place of honour for him in Paradise for every time he goes out in the morning or evening.*[213]

From Buraidah *radiyallaahu 'anhu*, who said that Allaah's Messenger (ﷺ) said: *Give the good tidings to those who walk frequently in the darkness to the mosques of perfect light on the Day of Resurrection.*[214]

---

[210] Reported by al-Bukhaaree (Eng. trans. 4/146/no.232) and Muslim (Eng. trans. 2/483/2204).

[211] Translator's note: A word usually used to signify guarding the frontier in *jihaad*.

[212] Reported by Muslim (Eng. trans. 1/157/no.485), Maalik, at-Tirmidhee and others.

[213] Reported by al-Bukhaaree (Eng. trans. 1/357/no.631), Muslim (Eng. trans. 1/325/no.1412) and others.

[214] Reported by Aboo Daawood (Eng. trans. 1/148/no.561) and at-Tirmidhee who described it as a *ghareeb hadeeth* and al-Haafidh al-Mundhiree said: "The narrators of its chain are reliable", and it is found in *Saheehut-Targheeb* (no.313).

From Aboo Hurairah *radiyallaahu 'anhu*, that Allaah's Messenger (ﷺ) said: *Indeed Allaah will provide a radiant light on the Day of Resurrection for those who frequently go to the mosques in darkness.*[215]

From Aboo Umaamah *radiyallaahu 'anhu*, who said that Allaah's Messenger (ﷺ) said: *Whoever goes out from his house in a state of purification to an obligatory Prayer then his reward is like that of a person making Hajj, in a state of ihraam. Whoever goes out to the optional Duhaa Prayer, taking the trouble for this alone then his reward is like that of a person performing 'Umrah. And a Prayer followed by a Prayer with no idle talk in between them is recorded in 'Illiyyoon.*[216, 217]

Also from Aboo Umaamah *radiyallaahu 'anhu,* that Allaah's Messenger (ﷺ) said: *There are three people in the safe keeping of Allaah: If he lives he is given provision and given sufficiency, and if he dies then Allaah will enter him into Paradise. Whoever enters his house and gives the greeting of 'Salaam' then he is under the safekeeping of Allaah. Whoever goes out to the mosque then he is under the safekeeping of Allaah. Whoever goes out (to fight) in the way of Allaah then he is under the safekeeping of Allaah.*[218]

From Salmaan *radiyallaahu 'anhu*, that Allaah's Messenger (ﷺ) said: *Whoever makes wudoo in his house, and perfects the wudoo, then comes*

---

[215] Reported by at-Tabaraanee in *al-Awsat* with *hasan* chain of narration, and it occurs in *Saheehut-Targheeb* (no.315).

[216] Translator's note: *'Illiyyoon* is the register of the righteous in the seventh heaven.

[217] Reported by Aboo Daawood (Eng. trans. 1/146/558) and is found in *Saheehut-Targheeb* (no.318).

[218] Reported by Aboo Daawood (Eng. trans. 2/689/no.2488) and Ibn Hibbaan in his *Saheeh* and it is found in *Saheehut-Targheeb* (no.319).

to the mosque then he is a visitor of Allaah's, and it is a right that the one who is visited should treat the visitor honourably.[219]

Points of benefit to be taken from these *ahaadeeth*:

(1) Walking to the Prayer raises one's rank and removes one's sins, both going and returning.

(2) That he is accredited with ten good deeds for every step he takes.

(3) The Muslim is written as being engaged in Prayer from the time he goes out from his house until he returns to it.

(4) The people who receive the greatest reward for the Prayer are those who have to walk the furthest, and then the next in distance after them.

(5) Each step which a person takes when walking to the Prayer is counted as charity for him.

(6) Taking many steps to the mosques is perseverance in obedience.

(7) That Allaah, the Most High, prepares a place of honour in Paradise for the servant for every time he goes out in the morning or the evening to the mosque.

(8) That Allaah, the Most High, will grant complete light on the Day of Resurrection to those who frequently walk in darkness to the mosques.

---

[219] Reported by at-Tabaraanee in *al-Kabeer* with two chains of narration one of which is good. It is found in *Saheehut-Targheeb* (no.320).

(9) That the reward for one who leaves his house in a state of purification to go out to the obligatory Prayer is like that of a person in a state of *ihraam* performing *Hajj*.

(10) That one who goes out to the mosque is under the safekeeping of Allaah, the Most High, Who will provide for and suffice him.

(11) That the person who walks to the mosque having perfected the *wudoo* goes out to visit Allaah, the Most High, and Allaah, the One free and far removed from all imperfections, showers blessings upon His servants by honouring those who visit Him, and that is by increasing their *eemaan*, their attentiveness in worship and their reward, and by raising their rank, removing distress from them and placing joy in their hearts.

22. The Excellence of Attachment to the Mosques and Sitting in them

From Aboo Hurairah *radiyallaahu 'anhu*, who said that I heard Allaah's Messenger (ﷺ) say: *There are seven whom Allaah will shade in His shade on the Day when there is no shade except His shade:*[220] *A just ruler; a youth who grew up in the worship of Allaah, the Mighty and Majestic;* ***a man whose heart is attached to the mosques****; two men who love each other for Allaah's sake, meeting for that and parting upon that; a man who is called by a woman of beauty and position, but he says: 'I fear Allaah'; a man who gives in charity and hides it, such that his left hand does not know what his right hand gives in charity; and a man who remembered Allaah in private and so his eyes shed tears.*[221]

From Aboo Hurairah *radiyallaahu 'anhu*, from the Prophet (ﷺ) that he said: *A man does not frequent the mosques for the Prayer and the remembrance of Allaah except that Allaah, the Most High, greets him joyfully, just as the family of one who is absent greet him with joy when he returns to them.*[222]

---

[220] i.e. the shade of His *'Arsh* (Throne) as occurs in the *hadeeth*: *Whoever gives respite to a person in straightened circumstances or remits his debts then Allaah will give him shade on the Day of Resurrection beneath the shade of His Throne, on the Day when there is no shade except His shade*. Reported by at-Tirmidhee who declared it *hasan saheeh* and it occurs in *Saheehut-Targheeb* (no.129).

[221] Reported by al-Bukhaaree (Eng. trans. 1/356/no.629), Muslim (Eng. trans. 2/493/no.2248) and others.

[222] Reported by Ibn Abee Shaybah, Ibn Maajah, Ibn Khuzaimah and others and it is found in *Saheehut-Targheeb* (no.315).

From Aboo Dardaa *radiyallaahu 'anhu*, who said that I heard Allaah's Messenger (ﷺ) say: *The mosque is the house of every pious person, and Allaah has granted comfort and mercy for everyone for whom the mosque is his house, and that they will traverse the bridge (as-Siraat) to Allaah's Pleasure and Paradise.*[223]

From 'Abdullaah ibn 'Amr *radiyallaahu 'anhumaa*, from Allaah's Messenger (ﷺ) that he said: *There are six sittings in which a person is guaranteed the safekeeping of Allaah, the Most High, as long as he is in one of them: In a congregational mosque; with a sick person; at a funeral; in his house; with a just ruler whom he supports and treats with respect; or at a place where people are fighting jihaad.*[224]

From Aboo Hurairah *radiyallaahu 'anhu*, who said: "Indeed there are those who are pillars for the mosques and there are angels who sit in their company. So if they are absent they ask after them, and if they are in need then they assist them."[225]

[223] Reported by at-Tabaraanee in *al-Kabeer* and *al-Awsat* and al-Bazzaar who declared it *hasan*, and it occurs in *Saheehut-Targheeb* (no.328).

[224] Declared *hasan* by Shaikh al-Albaanee in *Saheehut-Targheeb* (no.326) and is reported by at-Tabaraanee and al-Bazzaar.

[225] *Saheeh* as the saying of Aboo Hurairah *radiyallaahu 'anhu*, as occurs in *Saheehut-Targheeb* (no.327), reported by al-Haakim.

23. The Severe Warning Against Staying Away From the Congregational Prayer and the Effect Which it has in Reducing *Eemaan*

From Aboo Hurairah *radiyallaahu 'anhu*, who said that Allaah's Messenger (ﷺ) said: *I intended to give order for the Prayer to be established and order a man to lead the people in Prayer, and go with some men along with bundles of firewood to a people who do not present themselves for the Prayer and then burn their houses upon them with fire.*[226]

From Ibn Umm Makhtoom *radiyallaahu 'anhu*, who said that I said to the Prophet (ﷺ): *"I am aged and blind and my house is far from the mosque, and I do not have any guide to lead me, so do you find any concession for me?" He said: Do you hear the call? I said: "Yes." He said: I do not find any concession for you.*[227]

Also in a *hadeeth*: *A people will certainly desist from avoiding the congregational Prayers otherwise Allaah will set a seal upon their hearts and then they would be amongst the negligent.*[228]

From 'Abdullaah who said: "Whoever is pleased to meet Allaah tomorrow as a Muslim, then let him preserve in carrying out the five Prayers where the call is made for them, since they are from the paths of right-guidance, and it was Allaah who laid down the ways of right guidance for your

---

[226] Reported by al-Bukhaaree (Eng. trans. 1/350/617) and Muslim (Eng. trans. 1/315/1369), Aboo Daawood (Eng. trans. 1/144/548) and others.

[227] Reported by Aboo Daawood (Eng. trans. 1/145/552) and occurs in *Saheeh Sunan Ibn Maajah* (no.644).

[228] *Saheeh Sunan Ibn Maajah* (no.646) and it is reported by Muslim with the wording: '*the Jumu'ah Prayers.*'

Prophet. Certainly if all of you prayed in your houses then you would have abandoned the *Sunnah* of your Messenger, and if you abandoned the *Sunnah* of your Messenger you would have gone astray. I have seen the time when none of us would be absent from it except a hypocrite whose hypocrisy was well known, and I have seen the time when a man would be brought supported by two men until he joined the row."[229]

Points of benefit to be taken from these texts:

(1) The obligation of Prayer with the congregation.

(2) The Prophet (ﷺ) did not make concession for the aged, blind-man to stay away from the congregational Prayer, so how can there be any concession for the able bodied?

(3) That one who stays away from the congregational Prayer has been threatened with becoming one of the negligent and having his heart sealed.

(4) That staying away from the congregational Prayer without valid excuse is one of the signs of hypocrisy.

(5) The great striving of the Companions to be present at the congregational Prayers despite difficult circumstances.

---

[229] Reported by Aboo Daawood (Eng. trans. 1/144/550) and Ibn Maajah (no.777) and is found in *Saheeh Sunan Ibn Maajah* (no.644).

24. What Should be Done in Order to Arrive in Good Time for the Prayer

(1) We should read and comprehend the texts relating to the excellence of coming early to the Prayers.

(2) We should sleep early and not remain awake late into the night. Since there are some people who remain awake late at night and then miss the *Fajr* Prayer. Then one of them will perhaps return from work after *Dhuhr*, eat his lunch and then sleep due to tiredness. Then he may not get up for the *'Asr* Prayer, but rather have an extended sleep until close to sunset, and then quickly peck four *rak'ahs* for *'Asr* fearing that the sun is going to set upon him. Then when night comes he is unable to sleep early due to his having slept during the day. So he stays awake until sleeps overcomes him, and so he misses the *Fajr* Prayer again, missing praying it with the congregation and in its early time... this is the condition in which his life passes by.

(3) Advising one another to come in good time for the Prayer, especially the *Fajr* Prayer, making use of the telephone and so on.

(4) Using an alarm clock, and there are alarm clocks which repeat their alarm from time to time, and place them at a suitable distance so that you cannot switch them off before awaking properly.

(5) Reciting the various *adhkaar* for sleep, and this has a good effect in causing a person to wake up for *Fajr*.

(6) If the time for Prayer begins or is about to begin and you are engaged in some worldly business, then remember that the Hereafter has precedence, and if you are engaged in something connected with the Hereafter then remember that the best of good deeds is that you pray the Prayer

in its time. Furthermore beware of the Satan who holds out vain hopes and says: you have plenty of time, so complete your work.

(7) Know the times of Prayer and the time of *iqaamah*.

(8) Give importance to responding to the call of the *mu'adhdhin* and his saying: 'Come to the Prayer, come to success.'

25. The Excellence of Waiting for the Next Prayer After Having Prayed

From Aboo Hurairah *radiyallaahu 'anhu*, that Allaah's Messenger (ﷺ) said: *One of you does not cease to be in Prayer for as long as the Prayer withholds him, nothing preventing him from returning to his family except the Prayer.*[230]

In a narration: *One of you remains in Prayer for as long as the Prayer withholds him, and the angels say: 'O Allaah forgive him, O Allaah have mercy upon him', as long as he does not get up from his place of Prayer or break his state of purification.*[231]

From Anas *radiyallaahu 'anhu*, that one night Allaah's Messenger (ﷺ) delayed the *'Ishaa* Prayer until half the night had passed, then after completing the Prayer he turned and said: *The people prayed and slept, but you have not ceased to be engaged in Prayer for as long as you have been waiting.*[232]

From 'Abdullaah ibn 'Amr *radiyallaahu 'anhumaa*, who said: *"We prayed the Maghrib Prayer along with Allaah's Messenger (ﷺ), then whoever returned returned, and whoever remained remained, then Allaah's Messenger (ﷺ) came hurriedly, breathing heavily, and his knees were uncovered. He said: Receive good news. Your Lord has opened a gate from*

---

[230] Reported by al-Bukhaaree (Eng. trans. 1/355-356/no.628) and Muslim (Eng. trans. 1/322/1396).

[231] Reported by al-Bukhaaree (Eng. trans. 1/355/628).

[232] Reported by al-Bukhaaree (Eng. trans. 1/356/630).

the gates of the heavens and boasts of you to the angels, saying: 'Look at My servants, they have carried out an Obligatory (Prayer) and await the next.'[233]

From Jaabir ibn 'Abdullaah *radiyallaahu 'anhumaa*, who said that Allaah's Messenger (ﷺ) said: *Shall I not guide you to that by which Allaah wipes away evil deeds and removes sins? They said: 'Indeed yes, O Messenger of Allaah.' He said: Completing the wudoo when it is a hardship, taking many steps to the mosques, and awaiting the Prayer after the Prayer, that is persevering in obedience.*[234]

From 'Alee ibn Abee Taalib *radiyallaahu 'anhu*, that Allaah's Messenger (ﷺ) said: *Perfecting the wudoo when it is a hardship, walking upon foot to the mosques, and waiting for the Prayer after the Prayer greatly washes away sins.*[235]

From Aboo Hurairah *radiyallaahu 'anhu*, that Allaah's Messenger (ﷺ) said: *One who waits for the Prayer after the Prayer is like a warrior on horseback who strives hard fighting in Allaah's cause upon his horse against an enemy who bears a grudge against him. That is the greater perseverance in obedience (Ribaat*[236]*).*[237]

---

[233] Reported by Ibn Maajah and it occurs in *Saheehut-Targheeb* (no.425).

[234] Reported by Ibn Hibbaan in his *Saheeh* and it occurs in *Saheehut-Targheeb* (no.447).

[235] Reported by Aboo Ya'laa and al-Bazzaar with *saheeh* chain of narration. Al-Haakim declared it to be *saheeh* to the standard of Muslim and it occurs in *Saheehut-Targheeb* (no.449).

[236] Translator's note: A word usually used to refer to guarding the frontiers of Islaam.

[237] Reported by Ahmad and at-Tabaraanee in *al-Awsat* and the chain of narration of Ahmad is adequate as occurs in *Saheehut-Targheeb* (no.450).

From Ibn 'Abbaas *radiyallaahu 'anhumaa*, who said that Allaah's Messenger (ﷺ) said: *I saw my Lord*[238] *in the best appearance and He said to me: "O Muhammad!" I said: At your service O my Lord continually. He said: "Do you know what the highest company [of angels] are discussing?" I said: I do not know. So He placed His Hand between my shoulder blades and I found its coolness within my breast, or he said: in my chest, so I knew what was in the heavens and the earth*[239] *or he said: what is between the east and the west. He said: "O Muhammad! Do you know what the highest company are discussing?" I said: Yes, about the ranks, and those things which wipe away sins: walking on foot to the congregational Prayers, perfecting the wudoo in severe cold and awaiting the Prayer after the Prayer, whoever constantly performs them lives upon good and dies upon good, and is with regards to his sins just as the day his mother gave birth to him. He said: "O Muhammad." I said: At your service continually. He said: "When you pray, then say: O Allaah I ask you that I should do good, abandon evil and have love for the poor, and if you wish some trial for your servants then take me (in death) without being afflicted by it." He said: And the ranks are: spreading the (greeting of) salaam, providing food, and Prayer at night whilst the people sleep.*[240]

From Anas *radiyallaahu 'anhu*, from the Prophet (ﷺ) that he said: *Three are things which wipe away sins, three things are ranks, three things save, and three things cause destruction. So as for those which wipe away sins then they are: Perfecting the wudoo in severe cold, waiting for the*

---

[238] i.e. in a dream, and in a narration: "*someone came to me from my Lord*."

[239] Our Shaikh al-Albaanee says in *at-Targheeb*: "Meaning that which Allaah, the Most High, taught him regarding what they contained such as angels, trees and other things, and it is an expression of the breadth of the knowledge which Allaah gave to him, this is what is explained in *al-Mirqaat* (1/463)."

[240] Reported by at-Tirmidhee and is found in *Saheehut-Targheeb* (no.405).

Prayer after the Prayer, and walking on foot to the congregational Prayers. As for the ranks, then they are: providing food, spreading the (greeting of) salaam, and Prayer at night while the people sleep. As for those which save, then they are: justice when one is angry and when one is pleased, moderation when poor or when rich, and fear of Allaah in secret and in the open. As for those things which cause destruction, then they are: avarice which is obeyed, desires which are followed, and a persons having admiration for himself.[241]

From 'Uqbah ibn 'Aamir *radiyallaahu 'anhu*, who said that Allaah's Messenger (ﷺ) said: *The one sitting waiting for the Prayer is like one standing obediently in Prayer, and is written amongst those who are praying, from the time when he leaves his house until he returns to it.*[242]

Points of benefit that can be taken from these *ahaadeeth*:

(1) That the servant remains in Prayer for as long as the Prayer withholds him, and he is like one who is standing obediently in Prayer. He is written amongst the people who are praying from the time he leaves his house until he returns to it.

(2) The Angels supplicate for forgiveness and mercy for him as long as he remains at his place of Prayer and does not break his state of purification.

(3) Allaah, the Most High, opens a gate from the gates of the heavens and boasts to the angels of those who pray the *Maghrib* Prayer and then wait for the *'Ishaa* Prayer.

---

[241] Reported by al-Bazzaar, al-Baihaqee and others and it is *hasan* due to combination of its chains as occurs in *Saheehut-Targheeb* (no.453).

[242] Reported by Ibn Hibbaan in his *Saheeh* and reported by Ahmad and others in longer form and is found in *Saheehut-Targheeb* (no.454).

(4) Waiting for the next Prayer after having prayed greatly washes away sins.

(5) His status is that of a warrior on horseback who strives hard fighting in Allaah's cause against the enemy, and he is doing the greatest act of perseverance in obedience.

(6) Waiting for the next Prayer after having prayed is something about which the highest company of angels discuss, which shows its importance and worth.

(7) Waiting for the next Prayer after having just prayed is something which wipes away sins.

26. Some of the Benefits of *Khushoo'*[243]

[1] A lawful and good subsistence. Allaah, the Most High, says:

وَمَن يَتَّقِ ٱللَّهَ يَجْعَل لَّهُۥ مَخْرَجًا ۝٢ وَيَرْزُقْهُ مِنْ حَيْثُ لَا يَحْتَسِبُ

"Whosoever fears Allaah and keeps his duty to him, He will make a way for him to get out (from every difficulty). And He will provide him from (sources) he never imagine.[244]

[2] It causes a person to be as close as he can to his Lord, the One free of all imperfections and the Most High.

[3] It wipes away sins and brings about forgiveness of them.

[4] Success and well-being as Allaah, the Most High, says:

قَدْ أَفْلَحَ ٱلْمُؤْمِنُونَ ۝١ ٱلَّذِينَ هُمْ فِى صَلَاتِهِمْ خَٰشِعُونَ ۝٢

"Successful indeed are the believers. Those who offer their Prayers with humility and attentiveness (*khushoo'*)." [245]

[243] An abridgement of the proofs which have already been quoted along with their sources and I decided to repeat some of them for extra benefit.

[244] Soorah at-Talaaq (65):2-3

[245] Soorah al-Mu'minoon (23):1-2

[5] It forbids evil and wicked deeds.

[6] It increases one's guidance, Allaah, the Most High says:

وَٱلَّذِينَ جَٰهَدُواْ فِينَا لَنَهۡدِيَنَّهُمۡ سُبُلَنَاۚ

"As for those who strive hard in Us (Our Cause), We will surely guide them to Our Paths." [246]

[7] Entry into Paradise as occurs in the *hadeeth* which has preceded: *...then he has a guarantee from Me that I will enter him into Paradise.*

[8] Contentment of one's soul and joy, as he (ﷺ) said: *...Give the iqaamah for the Prayer. Give us comfort by it.* Also his (ﷺ) saying: *The Prayer was made the coolness of my eyes.*

[9] It causes the servant to reach the level of the foremost worshippers who worship Allaah as if they are seeing Him, as he (ﷺ) said: *Pray the Prayer of one who is bidding farewell, as if you were seeing Him.*

---

[246] Soorah al-'Ankaboot (29):69

Conclusion

This, O my Muslim brother, is the effect of the Prayer, and these are its benefits, so make your Prayer such that you pray with fear, humility and attentiveness so that Allaah, the One free of all imperfections, accepts it from you, and so that you may receive the fruits and benefits which spring from it, so that the society in which you live may change, such that *eemaan* becomes its foundation, and so that it adheres and clings firmly to the laws and regulations of Islaam.

May Allaah send praise, blessings and peace upon Muhammad, his family, his followers and his Companions.

Glossary

Aayah (pl. Aayaat): a Sign of Allaah; a verse of the Qur'aan.
Aayaat: See *Aayah.*
Aboo (Abee, Abaa): father of; used as a means of identification.
Adhaan: call to Prayer.
'Alaihis-salaam: "may Allaah protect and preserve him." It is said after the name of a Prophet of Allaah or after the name of an angel.
Ahaadeeth: See *Hadeeth.*
'Aqeedah: that which binds or that which is firmly rooted in the heart; the principles and details of belief.
Companions (Ar. *Sahaabah*): the Muslims who saw the Prophet (ﷺ) and died upon Islaam.
Da'eef: weak; unauthentic (narration).
Deen: way of life prescribed by Allaah i.e. Islaam.
Eemaan: faith; to affirm all that was revealed to the Messenger (ﷺ), affirming with the heart, testifying with the tongue and acting with the limbs. The actions of the limbs are from the completeness of *Eemaan*. Faith increases with obedience to Allaah and decreases with disobedience.
Fiqh: the understanding and application of the *Sharee'ah* from its sources.
Hadeeth (pl. **Ahaadeeth**): narration concerning the utterances of the Prophet (ﷺ), his actions or an attribute of his.
Hajj: Pilgrimage to Makkah.
Hasan: fine; term used for an authentic *hadeeth*, which does not reach the higher category of *Saheeh*.
Ibn: son of; used as a means of identification.
Ihraam: the clothes of the pilgrim while he performs *hajj* or *'umrah*.
Imaam: leader; leader in *Salaah*, knowledge or *fiqh*; leader of a state.
Iqaamah: second call to Prayer.
Isnaad: the chain of narrators linking the collector of the saying to the person quoted.

Jihaad: Striving; fighting in the cause of Allaah.

Jinn: A creation of Allaah created from smokeless fire.

Khilaafah: the Islamic state.

Kufr: Disbelief.

Masjid: mosque.

Mu'adhdhin: one who makes the *adhaan.*

Muharram: the first month of the Islamic calendar.

Nafl (pl. Nawaafil): An optional act; an act for which one is rewarded if it is done but one is not punished for if it is not carried out.

Radiyallaahu 'anhu/'anhaa/'anhum/'anhumaa: may Allaah be pleased with him/her/them/both of them.

Rahimahullaah/Rahimahumullaah: may Allaah bestow His mercy upon him/them.

Rak'ah: one cycle of the Prayer, consisting of standing, bowing and prostrating.

Ramadaan: the ninth month of the Islamic calendar during which Muslims are required to fast.

Rukoo': "bowing," a part of the Prayer.

Saheeh: correct; an authentic narration.

Salaam: the greeting used by the Muslims: *Assalaamu 'alaykum...*

Shaikh: scholar.

Shaitaan: Satan.

Sharee'ah: the Divine code of Law.

Shirk: associating partners with Allaah.

Sujood: "prostration," a part of the Prayer.

Sunnah: in its broadest sense, the entire *Deen* which the Prophet (ﷺ) came with and taught, i.e. all matters of belief, rulings, manners and actions which were conveyed by the *Companions*. It also includes those matters which the Prophet (ﷺ) established by his sayings, actions and tacit approval - as opposed to *bid'ah* (innovation).

sunnah: an action of the Prophet (ﷺ).

Soorah: a chapter of the Qur'aan.

Tafseer: Explanation of the Qur'aan.

Taqwa: "*taqwa* is acting in obedience to Allaah, hoping for His mercy upon light from Him and *Taqwa* is leaving acts of disobedience, out of fear of Him, upon light from Him."

Ummah: The Muslim nation.

'Umrah: the lesser pilgrimage (to Makkah).

Wudoo: the ablution (ritual washing) that is performed before the Prayer and certain other acts of worship.